THE CAMPUS CAMPAIGN GUIDE:

Winning A Student Political Office

By Kris R. Parker, Esq.

This is dedicated to my parents Thomas and

Carolyn Parker, who have always loved and

supported me unconditionally.

**THE CAMPUS CAMPAIGN GUIDE:
WINNING A STUDENT POLITICAL OFFICE**

Mascot Books
560 Herndon Parkway #120
Herndon, VA 20170
info@mascotbooks.com

PROPM1215A

Library of Congress Control Number: 2015915352

ISBN-13: 978-1-63177-378-5

Printed in the United States

www.mascotbooks.com

TABLE OF CONTENTS

Introduction 1

Chapter 1 — The Decision to Run 3

Chapter 2 — Understanding The Electorate 17

Chapter 3 — Campaign Timeline 29

Chapter 4 — Assembling a Core Staff 31

Chapter 5 — Raising Capital 41

Chapter 6 — Base vs. Waste 47

Chapter 7 — Assembling a Complete Team 67

Chapter 8 — Image 73

Chapter 9 — Platform Design & Strategic Plan 77

Chapter 10 — Endorsements 85

Chapter 11 — Campaign Materials 93

Chapter 12 — Message Delivery 101

Chapter 13 — Get Out the Vote 111

Conclusion 129

Introduction

The purpose of this book is to provide guidance to candidates aspiring for elected student positions. If you are interested in running for office at your school, but you lack the experience necessary and are unsure where to begin, this book is for you. The book will teach you fundamental campaign strategies and tactics, and will teach you how to apply them to a college, high school, or even middle school election through various examples and illustrations.

This book can be used to guide you through running for any elected student office, including student body or class president, student senate, or any elected position of a student organization. These campaign concepts can be used at any school level, including universities/colleges, high schools, and middle schools. And although some chapters may speak more to college campaigns, younger readers should use discretion as to which sections to apply to their campaign.

The book is organized in the chronological order of a political campaign. It begins with the decision to run and continues through each crucial step of the process, including the assembling of a campaign staff, and designing a platform that is both attainable and meets the wants and needs of the constituency for whom you will represent. This organization was designed to help guide you through the rigorous and often complex stages of running your first campaign. Use this book as a helpful resource in maneuvering through the unique campaign challenges that you will face.

Chapter 1 — The Decision to Run

The first obstacle in running for office is deciding if you should even run. Holding any office means that you are being entrusted by a group of people to represent their best interests. Whether the office is president of a student body of 50,000 or treasurer of a small tenth-grade class, the job comes with great responsibility and deserves the time and effort of sound judgment. You may be reading this book because you have already made the decision to run, and now you want to know what steps to take. Even if this is the case, it is wise to reassess your decision to assure that your logic is thorough. Please consider the following comprehensive factors and remember that the existence or non-existence of a single factor is typically not a reason to base your decision.

Positive Impact

A large percentage of students run for office simply because they want to improve the school or organization to which they belong. Clearly, it is important that you want to advance your school or organization, but it is imperative to look even further into the matter. Typically there are particular issues that a candidate wants to address, and the candidate should plan a campaign on addressing these issues and later implement a vision. At this point, a candidate should consider whether the implementation of these ideas are attainable, while considering that the typical term of any school office is one year or less.

Love for Alma Mater

Some students run for office because they have a strong emotional connection with their school. This can come from family tradition, or just plain old school spirit. Passion is an asset to any leader. It motivates them to do what is best for their school, and voters can sense when a candidate has that deep emotional tie with their alma mater. It is an intention not typically challenged, and although this connection can be an asset, it is only one factor.

A mind in a state of emotion can often be one that is clouded and unable make the difficult decisions required of a leader. Simply loving your alma mater does make you qualified to lead. All good student leaders have a loyalty to their school, but it is not the only reason they seek and hold office.

Personal Prestige

General Colin Powell once said, "Avoid having your ego so close to your position that when your position falls, your ego goes with it." Prestige is often associated with positions of power, and others may be impressed with a title, office, or accessibility to powerful people. Although it is a great feeling to be admired, it does nothing for your constituency. By making prestige the guiding factor of your decision to seek office, you realize that you are doing it for personal gain. If your decision puts your own interests before that of your electorate, you should not run for public office. If, however, you realize that prestige is a collateral effect of a low or unpaid job and you want to use that prestige to shine a positive light on the organization or institution to which you belong, then you should consider a possible run for office.

Resume

Are you running merely to improve your resume so that you are more attractive to graduate schools or to employers? Students must always be cognizant of career development and how that is reflected on their resume; yet, savvy employers will ask about your accomplishments while holding elected office. The people hiring new graduates have usually attended college themselves, and realize through experience that some of these positions are unopposed and that these resume entries can be just a veneer. Resume entries may get you in the interview room, but inevitably, you will have to answer questions about your legacy. If you are only running in order to make an entry on your resume, you could technically resign after the first day in office and include the position on your resume. This devalues the position, misleads employers, and is disingenuous to the voters, your volunteers, and yourself. Once more, putting yourself ahead of your constituents should make your decision very clear. A resume entry for holding office should be a badge of honor that shows that you not only worked to get elected, but that you served your school or organization in an honorable way. The resume benefit is another perk of a job that pays very little, if any. Look at it as a bonus, but not a deciding factor.

Popularity

For many, student office provides a social outlet. Leading people is a great way to get to know them. Other students or members who meet you while in the capacity of your position will receive an impression of you as a leader. Nonetheless, if you fail at your job and everyone's eyes are set on you, you may gain notoriety instead of popularity. Popularity is a potential benefit to holding student office, which can be enjoyed if you are successful fighting for your electorate.

Compensation

Some colleges/universities provide tuition wavers for stu-dents who serve in particular student offices, such as student body president or vice president. Other organizations may provide other financial incentives to its leaders, such as a waiver of membership dues. If you are having financial difficulty, which is common for college students, this perk can be enticing. These waivers are not likely put into place to incentivize running, but rather to make it possible for all students to have the opportunity to lead, regardless of their financial position.

Do you have what it takes?

Leadership Skills

Leadership is an art, not a science. It can be approached in many different ways. Some successfully lead through **Authoritative leadership**, giving little regard to the thoughts and feelings of their followers. These leaders take matters into their own hands and feel they know what is best for their followers and should not be questioned. Others lead by **Consultative leadership**. In this style, the leader gains the trust of their followers though healthy relationships of confidence and respect. Here, the leader cares about the ideas and feelings of their followers, and listens to them in order to assess their skills and preferences. Leaders use a diverse array of methods to achieve their goals; however, there are fundamentals that are essential in being an effective leader on any level.

There are two equal parts to being an effective leader: **Task Orientation** and **Relationship Orientation**. Although every situation calls for a different amount of each, both are equally important skills to possess throughout the duration of any leader's tenure. If a leader possesses a firm command of his/her surroundings and has a good understanding of the job, that leader will likely be respected. If a leader genuinely cares about his/her followers and works to create an honest bond with them, that leader will be liked. If a leader is respected and liked, the odds of that leader succeeding increase dramatically.

Task orientation requires a good understanding of both the big and small outlook of the organization. This skill is having a functioning understanding of both the substance and the process required to advance any agenda. If the president of the National Rifle Association knew nothing about guns or the legislative process, that president would likely fail. The coach of a basketball team should know the how to run a fast break or how to assemble a zone defense. Otherwise that coach will likely fail. Even if the coach learns these important elements throughout the course of the season, the team will suffer, and the coach's players and staff would have already lost confidence in their leader.

If a student runs for senator in the College of Science at your school, that student should probably know the key issues facing science students. The student should know the course requirements, the Dean's phone number, and how grades are calculated. Additionally, the candidate should know the processes required to get things done. This is the same for the campaign process. Hopefully, by reading this book, you will possess the task orientation required to run a campaign.

The consequences of not being task oriented are clear. If you do not fully understand your organization, its constituency, or its processes, your time will become consumed with overcoming a learning curve. This is time that is stolen from a limited term in office. Additionally, staff, constituency, and colleagues will not respect a leader who is not in full command of his/her surroundings. This can all be avoided by taking the time to study and understand the tasks required for the position you are considering to pursue. When you are task-oriented and your vision for success does not just include an end result, but how to get there, you will garner the respect required to lead. Although being respected is essential to all leaders, success is rarely achieved by respect alone. A well-rounded leader is not only respected, but is also liked by others.

Relationship Oriented—The other equally important half of a successful leader is relationship orientation. This is exactly what it sounds like. It encompasses the ability to build relationships with those around you, including your staff, constituency, and colleagues. By building friendly relationships, as opposed to merely working relationships, a bond will be created that will strengthen your leadership and enhance your experience.

Trust is built on a foundation of respect and likability. People will respect you as their leader if they believe you have a good understanding of what you want to do and how you plan to do it. Additionally, people will like you if they share a personal relationship with you. Humans, unlike computers, cannot simply be programmed to complete tasks. Relationships are a human quality and at their best, they can solidify the bond between a leader and his/her team, constituency, and colleagues.

Example: Alpha Pi Fraternity president, Justin, oversees a fraternity of 100 members. Among those 100 members are twelve core officers, including the community service director, Donnie. At a fraternity sponsored barbeque, Donnie introduces Justin to his parents. Instead of engaging with Donnie's parents and welcoming them to the function, Justin simply nods and continues grilling burgers. Later that week, Don invites Justin to a party at his apartment, but ignores the invitation because he would rather watch the baseball game on television with a few of his close friends. Soon thereafter, Justin contacts Donnie to inform him that he has a great idea for a service project and wants Donnie to get started on it in the next few days. Donnie, however, feels little obligation to go out of his way to help Justin, but instead has plans to go to the beach with some other fraternity brothers. As a result, Donnie goes to the beach and the project goes undone because Justin had other presidential responsibilities that weekend.

Justin clearly mishandled this situation. Although it may be true that Justin did not mean to snub his community service director, and it was technically outside the scope of their jobs, a strong leader would have taken this opportunity to get to know his officer. By reaching out to Donnie's family, Justin could have welcomed them and expressed his gratitude to them for all of their son's commitments and hard work. This would have likely gone a long way in building a relationship with Donnie. You must always consider people's motivations and incentives for working. If their motivation is simply to get paid or keep their position, will they do the same quality of work as someone motivated by the thought of pleasing the leader who they personally admire?

The caveat to building relationships is that they must be genuine. As most of us learn, relationships require commitment to giving, in addition to taking. A leader must show commitment to be available for situations which call for a friend. Good friends are available to listen to a friend vent or express thoughts in general. They are a helping hand during difficult times. This is what you have to be committed to give as a leader. When a leader does not genuinely care and is not committed to their followers, it becomes transparent, such as in the case of Justin and Donnie. Effective leadership calls for genuine commitment to relationship building, and not merely a facade or inconsistent efforts. The bond with your team is only as strong as your sincerity.

Imagine if Justin (president) would have accepted the invitation from Donnie (director) to come to the party. Yet, while at the party Justin was visibly uninterested and would have rather been watching the game with his friends. In this scenario, Justin may have made the situation worse. The other patrons at the party, including Donnie, would notice Justin's disinterest, which would send a clear message that he does not enjoy their presence and would rather be somewhere else. By not attending, Justin at least leaves the door open for interpretations. He may have wanted to come, but simply could not be there.

It is inevitable that a leader will be forced to interact with those people who he cannot naturally and immediately relate. And although there will be those who you do relate easily, one must not fail to attempt to build relationships with each and every person who you expect to follow you. If you build relationships with ninety-nine percent of your team and make no effort with the other one percent, you have still alienated a team member. When a member is alienated, that member will not only refuse to follow you, but they will likely harbor a disdain for you that can quickly spread. The potential harm caused by someone who is alienated is very difficult to overcome, regardless of the amount of support you enjoy. It is essential that a leader demonstrates the utmost respect and makes a genuine effort to build relationships with every member of the team.

Regardless of the diligence one may practice, there will always be situations where someone feels disrespected or even alienated. Whether or not this was intentional or even avoidable, a leader must confront it immediately and directly. By letting a situation linger and giving ill-feelings time to fester, you increase your chances of the situation spiraling outside of your control. As previously mentioned, this disdain can spread and become an even bigger problem. Your unhappy camper could build a coalition of those who begin losing confidence in your ability to lead. This can be avoided by assertively and tactfully confronting the situation with immediacy and directness. A wise man once said, "If you can't get everyone to like you, at least keep those who hate you far away from those who do not."

The first step is to understand how to be both task oriented and relationship oriented. The next step, which is equally as important and more difficult to implement, is understanding how to balance the focus of tasks and relationships. These components of leadership are like the two most important ingredients to a chef. Not every situation calls for both, and a good chef will know exactly when and how much to use each.

The basic rule of thumb is: Lower urgency situations call for a focus on relationship-orientation. Alternatively, when times call for getting immediate results, a leader must be more oriented on tasks. The more urgency present, the more task-orientation required. Trust is built on the foundation of respect and likability. The respect comes from your ability to get the job done, and likability comes from relationship building. As a leader, you will be put in a handful of situations that define you, and the goal is to have built a solid foundation of trust so that you and your team can successfully conquer those situations.

Example: An Army sergeant and a private are in a foxhole in Afghanistan taking gunfire from Taliban forces across a ridge. The two are behind a short wall, but fire is coming from each direction. The Sergeant knows the two must escape immediately. He notices an escape route which would require them to run about twenty yards under intense enemy gunfire. The sergeant decides that he will go first and needs the private to cover him with counter fire. The sergeant looks at the private, and in the midst of the deafening incoming gunfire says, "Private Wilson, how has your day been? Is your family doing well? You know, you have done a wonderful job in this war and your folks should be very proud that you left a great life to fly across the world to protect America's freedom. Right now, private, I have to ask you to do something for me. Thing is, I've got to run twenty yards with those angry fellows behind those rocks shooting at me. If you could, do you mind perhaps shooting back at them while I secure us an exit route? I know you are tired and if you don't want to do this, I understand. What do you say, private?

This is an extreme example and may seem amusing; nonetheless it makes a valid point. It is ridiculous to give orders this way in such an intense and life-threatening situation. Instead, the sergeant would have likely screamed loudly at the private, "Cover me!" and sprinted away without securing a response. The situation called for the highest of urgency imaginable, which required the sergeant to use his skills to complete the task of getting his troops out of danger. There was no reason for the sergeant to take the time to compliment and thank the private because time was of the essence. Hopefully, trust had been previously established between the two prior to being in this situation. If not, the private may not have stuck his neck out to cover the sergeant, or at least not done so with the confidence one would hope for when running into enemy fire.

Again, this example is extreme. Nothing says urgency like being shot at by an enemy. As the urgency of the situation decreases, the less absolute you should be in responding. For example, if the Taliban were throwing rocks at the soldiers instead of shooting assault rifles and were positioned about 200 yards further back, the sergeant could afford to be a bit less demanding. If instead of rocks, the enemies were hurling insults at the soldiers and they were positioned another 100 yards back, the sergeant could be even less demanding, and even use the situation to crack a joke with his inferior soldier to lend to his likability.

Example: Joe is the president of a community service organization and they are spending a Saturday afternoon building a swing-set at a foster home near their school. There is no deadline to get the project finished, and the foster home is very appreciative that the group is helping altogether. Joe is preparing to drive a nail when he realizes he cannot reach the hammer. The hammer is located on the ground beside the vice-president of the organization, April, who is busy sanding down the wood around the swings. Needing the hammer to drive the nail, Joe leans over into April's ear and at the top of his lungs screams, "Give me the damned hammer!!!" April was caught off guard and as a result of her reaction, bumped her head on the swing set. Understandably, April was confused, embarrassed, and even injured by Joe's unnecessary demand for the hammer.

Clearly, this is another extreme example and it is clear that Joe handled this situation miserably. The example, nonetheless, illustrates the point that when urgency is low, a leader should consider the thoughts and feelings of his or her teammates. There was no urgency whatsoever and this was a good opportunity for Joe to get to know his team and to make them feel comfortable around their leader. Instead of hastily demanding the hammer from April, he could have asked April how her sanding was going and maybe check to see if she needs a water break. There was no urgency to get the project finished, so why not build some relationship capital with your team so that they enjoy the experience and their time with you?

Let us add some urgency to this insouciant example. Consider that the deadline for completing the swing set was the end of the day. The foster home took out a city permit to build the swing set and the permit dictated that construction had to be completed on that day at 5:00 P.M. sharp. This slightly changes the situation because it now includes some urgency. And although it is still not the same level of urgency as taking enemy gun fire, it does increase the amount of focus on getting the task completed, and lowers the focus on building relationships. Instead of asking April how she is doing or if she needs a break, Joe could simply say, "April, please give me the hammer." If there was even more urgency, Joe may not even say "please", but just "April, give me the hammer." There is no scenario conceivable that would call for Joe yelling and cursing at April.

The situations you will encounter as a leader will not likely be this extreme. The skill of learning to balance these two priorities is a skill that you will be perfecting throughout every leadership endeavor in your career. If you can conclude right away that you are unable or unwilling to build relationships with people who you may have little in common, running for an office may not fit your skill set. If you know that you are unable or unwilling to sternly and tactfully confront someone in an urgent situation, you may not want to pursue a leadership role. Hopefully, this chapter has provided you with enough information to assist you in making that decision.

It is strongly recommended that you carefully examine each of the listed considerations for running for student office. It is also suggested that you list all of these factors, and write down how each will affect your decision whether or not to run. Remember, all of the above factors are valid if considered collectively; yet not one factor should be considered exclusively. After you write your status under each of these considerations, take it and review it carefully. Perhaps even review it with a relative or trusted friend in order to get a different perspective. This is a very important decision that will drastically affect you and possibly many others. It deserves the utmost consideration.

If you have considered all of the factors and you have decided to throw your hat into the ring, it's time to get to work on organizing your campaign!

Chapter 2 — Understanding the Electorate

Before you can assemble a staff or draft a platform, you have to take time to examine the students who will potentially vote in your election. Throughout this book, you will repeatedly see the term "demographic." This term refers to the statistical character of a population. Some examples of general demographics are gender and race. More specific demographic examples would be employment or marital status. The more specific your data, the more equipped you will be to draft an effective platform. If you are running for senator for the College of Liberal Arts, it is important that you understand the identity of the Liberal Arts students and the many groups that make up that constituency. If, however, you are running for student body president, you will have to cast a much wider net, which will take more time and effort to analyze.

A good campaigner assumes nothing. By assuming that your ideas will garner the votes needed to win your election, you are unnecessarily rolling the dice and risking the investments made by you and others. Voters are looking for solutions to problems they already have. When you identify these issues, you open yourself a good channel of communication to use during the campaign. Take the time to do the research, to find out who your voters are and what issues are most important to them. This chapter is designed to direct you in that research, so that you can be efficient with this valuable time leading up to your election.

Magnifying Glass

Imagine you are looking at a map on Google Earth. At first you see the entire globe, but each time you click on the globe, you take a closer look at the location you chose. Eventually, you can go all the way down to the ground level. This is where we get the term "grass roots." When assessing your electorate, you will take the same approach. First you want to see the electorate as a whole, and see what general demographics make up the electorate. Once you have made these general determinations, you will want to dig deeper and take a closer look at each demographic to get more specified information on that group. The deeper you are able to dig, the more information you will begin to collect about potential voters.

Although more specific demographics will change based on where you are and what kind of office you are chasing, general demographics will typically remain the same. Below is a list of some of the general demographics you should consider when doing your research.

Gender — This is probably the most general of all demographics. Often times there are issues and candidates who relate more to one gender over another. It's valuable to know what the ratio is, especially if there is an extreme lean one way or the other. Consider that many of today's colleges were once segregated based on gender, and today's enrollment numbers may reflect a staggered number of males or females. If a college has the women to men ratio of nine to one, an uninformed campaigner may run on an issue which targets male votes while ignoring ninety percent of the electorate.

Age — This may not be such an important consideration in high schools or middle schools, but in colleges age identification is essential. Colleges are becoming more and more nontraditional in regards to age. This is especially true at commuter and community colleges, where students often attend part-time or evening classes. And although these students may not be very active in extracurricular college activities, they will vote if you can persuade them that there are incentives.

Ethnicity — Minority students often share interest in distinct issues that other students may not have considered. It should also be considered that most schools have exchange student programs, and these students are often willing to become involved in the election process while in this country. It may feel awkward and even wrong to profile certain races, but it is important to know what issues are facing these students so that you can reach out them. Universities are working hard to encourage minorities to attend colleges, and at many universities minorities are a growing demographic that could make or break your bid for office.

Religion — Students affiliate with a wide assortment of religions. And within most religions are denominations with slightly different beliefs. Traditionally, Christians have made up a majority of students. Today, however, there is much more diversity of religions, and even organizations that express non-belief in religion. Religion is a very sensitive topic and by understanding your schools religious make-up, you can open effective lines of communication with interested and passionate voters. Adversely, ignorance of this demographic could prove disastrous due to its sensitive nature.

Organization Affiliation — A student's voter identity can often be defined by what group(s) they are affiliated. A student's organizational affiliation provides a window to a student's beliefs and values. It not only shows what they are interested in, but it shows what they are passionate about. Student athletes, for example, are consumed with a rigorous schedule full of classes, practices, and training. You know right away these students are passionate about athletics. You know that they appreciate any support school leaders can give them to be successful. Unlike many of the other demographics, student organizations are structured and usually meet weekly during the school year. This presence of organization makes it easier for you to communicate and understand this essential demographic.

Greek organizations usually play a big part in college/university elections, and can be complex to understand. If you determine that fraternity and sorority organizations play a big role in student life on your campus, you should consider taking a closer look at their issues and concerns. It is important not to yield to personal feelings when it comes to Greek organizations. Some non-Greeks harbor ill feelings toward fraternities and sororities, and attempt to win without them. On the other hand, candidates who are Greek may attempt to depend solely on the Greek community to win an election. Regardless of your feelings, Greeks can play a big part in your election because they are already organized, they share common beliefs, and they are easily mobilized. If you are a member of a fraternity or sorority, be aware that non-Greeks will be alienated by a campaign that is exclusive to Greek members. Lastly, never join a Greek organization just to run for office. Your intentions will be transparent and voters may question your integrity. This often backfires when the members learn that you were less than sincere when taking their oath of brotherhood or sisterhood. You can win the Greek vote without being Greek by carefully understanding what this population wants, and being effective at convincing them you are the person will best represent them.

Areas of Study — If you are running a campus-wide office, it is imperative to know what areas of study most students are participating. This will help you understand what their needs may be. If a majority of students at a college are studying business, the candidate should be very familiar with the current issues facing the business school. Someone's area of study is a good indicator of the interests and passions of large groups of your electorate.

Political Affiliation — This demographic typically carries less weight in a high school or middle school election, but on a college campus it could have some bearing. This is especially true in extreme situations. Be aware of any drastic political leanings your electorate might possess. Party politics can be unnecessarily divisive and off-putting to many college students. So while it is important to know the political landscape of your school, try to distance yourself from petty and unpopular politics whenever possible.

There are thousands of different types of demographics and intra-demographics. The ones listed are general and should be assessed in order to take a deeper dive. The deeper and more precise the effort you exert at this level, the more targeted your platform can be. If a platform issue is designed to attract a very particular crowd, that crowd will likely be motivated to cast a vote for you. And the bigger that target crowd, the better your chance of winning.

At this point, you are likely asking the question: Where and how do I get this information? This can be tricky because every school is different. If you are on a college campus, you will likely have an office on campus for institutional research. This office is designed to gather statistical data about the university, and they may be willing to share information with you if you ask. For high schools and middle schools, you should check with your school's administrators to see if any data is available. If you are unable to acquire statistical information, do not get discouraged. You will likely have to collect your own information by using whatever means available.

If you are on a college campus, see your dean of students. Chances are that this office will have valuable information about the demographics of your school, and the dean's office should be very willing to assist you. Also consider scheduling a meeting with the director of student affairs on your campus. If they cannot give you concrete statistics, they can at least give you a general outlook which will give you a good jumping-off point. You can also speak with different administrators for information on different demographics. For instance, to get information on students who live on campus, you should talk with the school's director of residential housing. For athletics, you could meet with the athletic director. If you find that your options are limited, remember to keep asking questions and keep your ear to the ground. A dean of students should be able to lead you to the appropriate offices to obtain the demographical information needed to proceed with more specific data. If you exert the effort and avoid uneducated guesses, the information will likely be available for your benefit.

Example: At Hypo College, Natalie is running for SGA president. Hypo has an enrollment of just over 10,000 students. By conducting some preliminary research, Natalie discovers that Greeks make up 90% (9,000) of the school's enrollment. A novice campaigner may stop here and begin crafting a platform designed to simply cater to general Greek issues; a more experienced campaigner, however, will peel another layer from the onion. Imagine Natalie is a savvy campaigner and learns that of those 9,000 students that are Greek at Hypo, only 15% (1,350) are in fraternities compared to 85% (7,650) who are in sororities. This changes things dramatically, but when she dug even deeper into

Hypo's population of sorority girls, she found that 70% of these girls (5,355) live off-campus and commute to Hypo. Now, instead of crafting a platform to address a 90% Greek enrollment, Natalie is equipped with much more information. She knows that over half of Hypo's enrollment is made up of sorority girls who commute to school. Natalie has identified 53% of the total enrollment who share three distinct demographics. With this knowledge, Natalie can craft a campaign platform to reach directly to these students.

It is very tempting to stop researching and begin drafting a campaign plan by simply assuming what issues are important to the demographics identified. This is especially true when you have identified a narrowed demographic like the one in the previous example. Natalie identified that over 50% of Hypo's enrollment are sorority girls who commute to school. It would be tempting for Natalie to just assume that she could reach this particular voting block by talking about implementing more social activities or a shuttle for transporting commuter students who park off-campus. Because Natalie failed to finish her research, she did not discover a very critical concern with sororities. In the past four months, twelve girls have been assaulted in their sorority house and in sorority parking lots. Campus sororities are terrified about the recent outbreak of violence. Knowing this, your social events and shuttle idea seem miniscule since the girls are seeking immediate security. This could have been prevented by a single phone call to sorority leadership.

Listening Tour

The next step is reaching out to these important demographics to explore what issues are important to them by going on a "listening tour." If you fail to include this step, you only assume that you already know their concerns, and you make an unnecessary assumption that can easily be avoided. A good candidate will take the time to visit and listen to groups of students to understand what issues are important enough to motivate them to go to the polls. In addition to understanding the issues, you are also working towards building recognition and credibility.

Some groups are easier to reach than others. If a targeted group fits nicely into an organization (like in Natalie's example), you can simply call the leaders of these groups and ask to have a discussion. If these groups are not already organized, it may require a more creative approach. For example, say you are running for class president of your high school and you discover that there is a demographic of students who live in one neighborhood, which is located 15 miles from the high school. These students stick together and rarely socialize with other students. Since they are not technically organized, it may be impossible to address all of them or to meet with the leader of their group. However, with a little bit of work, you could probably identify someone who unofficially leads the group and have a conversation with that person. You could even take some time to make the long bus ride to their neighborhood after school and find out what kinds of things are important to them. Campaigning requires creativity and the willingness to reach out to people with whom you may not normally socialize.

When reaching out to these groups or group leaders, it's important to be open about what you are doing. At this point, you probably have not made yourself an official candidate, so you should inform them that you are considering a run at office and you are doing some research to find out what issues are important to students. If you are opaque about your intentions, it will likely show. And even if you are able to deceive them initially, they will put things together when they see you running for office down the road. People typically assume that all "politicians" lack integrity, so you will likely be fighting an uphill battle to earn trust. Being dishonest to anyone, especially a key constituency, is no way to start a campaign.

Remember that when you are talking to these chosen demographics, you are not campaigning. Most campuses limit the period for when students can campaign. It is a good idea to check your school's bylaws for a definition of "campaigning." If there is no definition available, speak with the appointed election commissioner or an advisor to your schools student government and memorialize the discussion for your records. Furthermore, use common sense when meeting with these groups. Do not wear or distribute campaign paraphernalia of any kind, and do not ask for anyone's vote. Remember, you will be back to do this later. This is simply an opportunity to listen, not to sell your candidacy.

Another good way to insert yourself into the informational loop of your chosen demographics is to attend open events. Many organizations will hold social events, panel discussions, or even open meetings. Check your school's newspapers and bulletins to see when and where these events are occurring. Organizations usually post events on their website or on a social networking site. Insert yourself into those circles whenever possible. Your main goal here is to listen in order to understand the issues facing students at your school. It never hurts to be seen and recognized at these events, but your main goal is to listen, take good notes, and be honest about why you are there. This is especially true if you are attending events with sensitive interests such as a religious organization or a social justice group. It is a big advantage if you are already a member of a targeted group; however, do not join the organization just because you need their vote. Critics will question your integrity and motives for every decision you make, so approach each choice very carefully.

Another good way to keep your ear to the ground is to regularly read publications. Take fifteen minutes every morning to read the school newspaper, the local newspaper, bulletins, or even emails to understand important issues. If you already have people who are willing to help you, you could delegate some of these to them. A helper could scan assigned publications and bulletins for you to collect information that could include valuable for you to review each day. Save these clippings so that you can refer back to them with your staff later in the process. If your school has a radio station, keep it on while driving or in the gym so that you always have your ear to the ground.

Lastly, you can find out important issues by polling students. This process can be extremely time consuming and if not done professionally, will not be scientific. Polling is not usually effective if you poll the general campus population because you will get hundreds of different interests that will be impossible to timely digest. Do your primary research on the front end, and then apply the poll to the groups you have already identified. By asking open-ended questions, you could discover concerns that you were not already aware of. You could then take more time to ask other students if the concerns you found are wide-spread concerns. You could conduct a poll or survey with a comment box, or by simply passing out questionnaires on campus. Also consider using polling tools on the internet to get unfiltered opinions from core constituencies.

At this point, you have made a calculated decision to run for office, you have identified the demographics that can get the votes needed to win, and you have identified the key issues and concerns of those chosen demographics. Now that you are equipped with this valuable information, it is time lay out a campaign plan, which begins with an effective timeline.

Chapter 3 — Campaign Timeline

In order to manage the overwhelming tasks required to be completed during a campaign, it is important to strategically compartmentalize the time remaining. Each of your core staff members should have access to a uniform calendar. The calendar should be done electronically, so that it can be altered periodically by the campaign manager. This is also helpful in that core staffers can access the master calendar in the field with smart phones and tablets.

When placing dates on the schedule, first consult the election by-laws. There are important dates such as a filing deadline, a date for the campaign to actually begin, and the date(s) of your election. After that, insert the dates of important campus events. This could include organizational functions, sporting events, or any other events in which you will need to prepare.

The calendar is also a good way to set deadlines for completing essential campaign tasks. If deadlines are set and enforced, more will get accomplished. When deadlines and goals are not set, there is a lack of urgency; which can serve as motivation for your team. Some examples of calendar deadlines are: deadline to complete all campaign signs and fliers, deadline for meetings with all organizations, and a deadline for raising the funds needed to launch your campaign. The core staff should work together to set these initial dates and periodically add to the master calendar when needed.

Deadlines are set by working backwards from election day. Your election by-laws will likely dictate that the time-frame for campaigning will last no longer than a few weeks, and voting will take place in one or two days. The goal is to have everything in order for the first day of campaigning. This does not suggest that your deadline for everything should be on the first day of campaigning. For instance, you should give yourself a deadline to assemble your core staff. Once the staff is assembled, you should set deadlines for crafting a platform; and then a later deadline for assembling your campaign marketing materials. As you continue to meet these goals, you will move closer to being prepared for the upcoming campaign stretch.

In order to decide how much time will be allotted to these tasks, consider a few different factors. First, work your way back from the first day of the campaign period to see how many days you have. Next, take into consideration how much time is reasonable to get each task accomplished with the resources available. The earlier you are able to make your decision and secure a core staff, the more time you will have to space out these deadlines. Adversely, if you procrastinate, you will put yourself and your staff at a disadvantage with condensed deadlines. While urgency can be used as a tool to motivate your team, too much urgency can cause a lack of focus that can lead to avoidable mistakes.

A campaign calendar is an important tool that all staffers should have access to and be reminded about daily. It should contain key dates for events and deadlines to motivate the team to get campaign tasks accomplished, and to be ready for the campaign period and election.

Chapter 4 — Assembling a Core Staff

Regardless if you are organizing a campaign on the college, high school, or middle school level; and regardless of what office you seeking, it is essential that you assemble a core team who can help put your plan into action.

It is necessary to put your most important pieces in place first. When building a house, you first lay a dependable foundation so that the house stands firm. In a campaign, your campaign manager is your foundation and should be put into place before any other parts. If you are running for president of an organization, class, or student body, you may be required to run with a vice-president. If this is the case, you should select your vice-president next. After your campaign manager and vice-president (if needed), select a finance director, often referred to as a treasurer, in order to manage the campaign's fiscal matters. These positions make up a core staff and will do the majority of the lifting throughout the campaign. Any deviation from this order could potentially harm the stability of your campaign's organizational structure and cause avoidable mishaps along the way.

Campaign Manager

The most important position in any campaign is the campaign manager. The manager is the brains of the operation and tells the rest of the body when, where, and how to work. There should never be a campaign issue, meeting, or concern that does not involve the campaign manager. The manager will handle all operations of the campaign, including but not limited to: assisting the candidate in assembling a staff, scheduling and running meetings, arranging and managing campaign events, communicating with the candidate on a daily basis, and assessing and solving problems on a daily basis. Below is a list of qualities and factors you should consider when selecting a campaign manager.

Trust — The number one consideration for selecting a campaign manager is trust. A candidate confides in a manager about everything, and if a manager is not fully trusted, the candidate may withhold crucial information that a manager needs to guide the campaign. You must be sure that you trust that the manager is committed to the hard work and the long hours required to be successful. Ideally, you will already have a relationship with the person you choose and trust will have already been established. Since time is of the essence, both parties must be in task mode and not interrupted by trying to build a personal relationship and hiring a staff simultaneously.

Compatibility — You and your campaign manager should have good chemistry, and communication should be nearly effortless. The candidate and the manager will talk daily, and the more easily and efficiently they communicate, the more productive the campaign will be. At certain times during a campaign, the manager is the only staffer who can challenge the candidate's position with brutal frankness. And without trust and compatibility, this interaction could be toxic to the relationship. If the candidate and the manager have fundamental differences in philosophy and are not compatible, it must be discovered before a candidate is selected.

Competence — A good campaign manager will have a firm

grasp on the election process and how each staff member's duty is performed. The manager is often delegated the freedom to manage campaign staff, thus knowledge and strong leadership skills are essential qualities.

Thick Skin — Softies need not apply. A good manager is able to dish out the criticism, and take criticism, without it becoming personal. Elections happen quickly, and time spent pandering to one another's feelings is time that could be spent winning votes.

Sound Judgment — The manager will make independent decisions for the campaign on a daily basis. You will need someone who is a problem solver and who can react quickly. It is also important that your chosen manager is proven in making calculated decisions, since he/she will be assisting you in selecting and managing the campaign staff.

Time Management — The manager will be required to multi-task. It takes a special student to juggle being a campaign manager with classes, studies, and the normal life of a student. You should be sure your chosen campaign manager is aware and ready for the challenge.

Though it is important not to guarantee positions on your staff after the campaign, a successful campaign manager will make the ideal candidate for your chief- of-staff once in office. If the campaign manager is successful during the campaign, that student would be ready to hit the ground running as chief-of-staff. There is not a better audition for managing a staff like running a successful campaign.

As you will learn in the next section, candidates should consider electability when selecting members of their staff. When selecting a campaign manager, however, electability is less of a consideration due to the fact that the manager often works behind the scenes. It is preferred not to have anyone on your staff, especially at a high level, who may be damaging to the image of your campaign.

Vice President

Selecting a vice-president may not be necessary, depending on the office you are seeking and your school's requirements. When running for the office of president of any institution, a vice president is usually included. Some schools require vice-presidential candidates to run their own separate campaign, but others require the vice-president run with the presidential candidate. If the office you are seeking does not require you to run with a vice president, skip ahead to the next chapter.

Like the decision of selecting a campaign manager, selecting a good vice-president can make or break your campaign. While the campaign manager operates as the nerve center of the campaign, the vice-president's role is representational and cosmetic. The vice-president must appeal to the voters you are targeting. Choosing a vice-president requires a very different list of considerations for you and the campaign manager to consider. These considerations are known as the Four C's, and are listed below.

Counterbalance — The ideal vice-presidential candidate will balance the ticket. This means that your vice-presidential candidate should have the ability to attract the targeted demographics which are difficult for you to reach alone. Always choose someone who brings something new to the table of electability. By choosing someone from the same mold as you, and who runs in the same circles as you run, you limit the amount of voters your campaign can reach. Alternatively, you expand the number of voters to whom you can relate, giving your campaign an expanded range.

Choosing a close friend can be tempting when selecting a vice president. There is already a high level of trust, and you are likely compatible. Although this established trust is encouraged when selecting a campaign manager, it is not a principal consideration when selecting a vice-president. Friends likely have many of the same acquaintances, and they are likely involved in the same groups, organizations, and even classes. When you select a close friend for your vice presidential candidate, you will likely appeal to the same voters, and your electoral reach becomes limited. A friend's trust and compatibility does not overcome the limitation you place on your campaign by failing to extend your reach to new demographics. If you were choosing teams for a pick-up basketball game, you would likely choose your friends. If losing the game, however, meant losing a large sum of money, a semester of college life, and countless hours of stress and heartache, you probably would reconsider. Select the person who can get the job done.

Example: Albert told his best friend and fraternity brother that, during his upcoming senior year, he would run for student body president. His friend, Josh, agreed; and Josh said he would be Albert's vice-president. The two often joked about this scenario and how exciting it would be if the two of them were elected. During their senior year, Albert did indeed run for president. He was contacted by Josh, who inquired about their past plans of running together. As lifelong friends, the two ran together as they had always dreamed. Since they were fraternity brothers who practically knew all of the same people, they were unable to reach out to a large number of voters. The ticket of Albert and Josh had great appeal to about 4% of the campus. Josh did not bring anything new to the ticket. Although Albert can trust and communicate well with Josh, he was unable to reach out to new voting groups with Josh as his selection.

Credibility

Your vice-president is an extension of you. This person is in the public eye, and must be trusted to represent the campaign and its efforts in a respectful manner. If elected, the vice-president fulfills a one-year term and usually can only be removed by a lengthy legislative proceeding. Most student governments or organizations' constitutions follow the US Constitution, which requires an impeachment procedure to terminate a vice-president. Put simply, you probably will not have the power to fire you vice-president after elected. Thus, you should be sure that your selection is credible.

Competency

The vice-president must always be ready to assume the top office with little or no notice given. Thus, the student selected should possess the fundamental leadership skills needed to succeed. Most constitutions require the vice-president to preside over the legislative branch of the organization. Whether a student senate, a fraternity board, or a council overseeing a group; the vice-president should be familiar with parliamentary procedure. Legislative bodies play a major part in the implementation of a president's agenda. If the vice-president leads a legislative body but is unfamiliar with its procedures, it will be difficult to advance that agenda. A competent vice-president will be familiar with Robert's Rules of Order, which provides the fundamentals of parliamentary procedure.

Compatibility

It is likely that a president and vice-president will be working together daily, appearing publicly together, and talking repeatedly about important issues. Both the presidential candidate and the vice presidential candidate must stay on message with the targeted voters. The vice-president should feel strongly about the issues, and be dedicated to staying on message throughout the campaign. Chemistry is vital in being able to analyze the daily challenges arising throughout your campaign. If there is no history of working together or no sign of chemistry, it is wise to keep looking.

Use the Four C's to evaluate your candidates' credentials for the job of vice-president. To assist you further in this decision, you should score each candidate in all four areas in order to get a better understanding of each candidate's strength. Below is an example of a table to use for measuring each candidate in all four areas. The score uses a scale from one through ten, with the perfect score of forty. You can even change the scoring system and add more points to areas you feel are more valued to your particular selection.

Sample VP Selection Chart

	Counterbalance	Credibility	Competency	Chemistry	Total
Amber	9	9	7	7	32
Bobby	4	8	6	9	27
Carissa	8	7	7	7	29
Darren	5	8	6	9	28
Emily	7	7	6	6	26

When selecting a vice-president, make sure you develop a philosophy to your search. Simply choosing a friend or who someone popular may not be enough. Although these are important factors, they are not dispositive. The recommended factors are listed, but there may be more depending on your constituency. This is a very important decision that demands your utmost attention and thought. A mistake here can cost you the election, so hunker down make a good selection.

Finance Director (Treasurer)

The last core position to select is your finance director, sometimes known as the treasurer. Although some campaigns will require more funding than others, you should always have someone to manage funds being raised and funds being spent. Colleges, high schools, and middle schools usually include a spending limit in order to keep money from being a factor in seeking student office. As a result, your campaign will likely be audited to ensure that you stay within the limit. A treasurer will educate themselves on the school's spending policy and work to make sure that members of your campaign staff understand these rules. The treasurer will implement a campaign policy for how money comes in and out, in order to comply with the requirements. A mistake in this area could risk all of the hard work put into the campaign by you and your staff.

Trust, compatibility, and competency are also important qualities in selecting a treasurer. Understandably, a competent treasurer will know how to keep the financial books for the campaign. But in addition to that, this person will be able to track down the applicable rules that apply to your campaign, and have the ability to educate the rest of the staff on those rules. Furthermore, a competent treasurer will be creative and innovative enough to incorporate an effective system for raising and spending money so that you, your manager, and your vice-president will not have to consume valuable campaign time worrying about finances. Choose someone who is meticulous, and not afraid to enforce the financial policies put into place. This person needs to be willing to step in at any time to ensure complete compliance with spending rules.

When selecting core team members, be careful not to burn the bridges of those you did not select. If you choose not to select someone, yet that person could still be a good addition to your staff in a different area, be sure to convey to them that you want them to serve in a different capacity. Without a tactful rejection, you might motivate this person to support another candidate and work against you. Later, you will be assembling an entire staff; and since you will likely not be limited on the size of your staff, you can include everyone and even create meaningful titles for each of them. When workers have a title, they know they are a formal part of the campaign and they will take ownership.

Now that you have assembled a core staff, it is time to raise capital. The next chapter will discuss how to raise the money needed to sustain an efficient campaign.

Core Staff Checklist:

✓ *Campaign Manager*
✓ *Vice President or running mate (if needed)*
✓ *Finance Director (Treasure)*

Chapter 5 — Raising Capital

A political campaign is about marketing ideas and positions. Unfortunately, effective marketing is not free. As previously discussed, schools often limit the amount of money a campaign can spend to insure an even playing field for candidates. Though the United States Supreme Court has ruled that such restrictions are unconstitutional as a violation of one's first amendment right to free speech, the U.S. Court of Appeals for the Ninth Circuit has ruled that colleges can enforce such limits as part of its police power. The cost of a campaign depends on the office you are seeking, the spending limit required in the election by-laws, and the competitive nature of your particular campaign.

Before making any effort to raise money, you and your finance director should consult the by-laws for a spending cap rule. If there is a cap and you expect a competitive election, it would be advantageous to attempt the raise the full amount allowed. Money can be returned to the donor in the event that it is not needed. You never want to be forced to halt your campaign to raise more funds. By raising the maximum amount you are allowed to spend, you will not have to concern yourself with fundraising and can concentrate on reaching voters.

In addition to checking the by-laws for spending rules, you and your finance director should also consult the person administering the election, usually the election commissioner, to get an explanation of the spending rule. Find the person who will be making the decision if a campaign rule is challenged. If possible, get their interpretation of the rule in writing. Election by-laws can be vague, and it is wise to clear up any ambiguities early in the process to avoid confusion. For instance, does the spending cap address donations? Do those donations count towards the spending cap? Additionally, what exactly is the definition of "campaign spending?" If you purchase pizzas for a sign making party at your dorm room, does this constitute campaign spending? Are there restrictions on fundraising? If you are unable to get clear answers on your questions, err on the side of caution.

Once you and your finance director have internalized the campaign spending rules, it's time to raise some dough. As mentioned before, the amount of money needed will vary depending on the office you are running for, and the election rules. If you need to raise only a small amount, consider funding it yourself or speaking with your immediate family members about donating. Higher offices could require raising an amount that is outside your ability to self-finance. This may require opening a campaign bank account and making a fundraising plan.

At this point, you should have a campaign manager, a finance director, and possibly a vice-presidential candidate. These campaign officers will be beneficiaries of a campaign victory, and you should not hesitate to solicit their help in raising the funds needed to compete. Give each core staffer a fundraising goal, with you assuming the biggest portion of the goal. Meet with members to craft a plan for how they will raise their portion. Consider asking members of your family, close friends, and possibly neighbors. No one wants you to succeed more than your friends and family. A professionally written fundraising letter to family and friends will project to them that you are committed and professional. Your letter should include what office you are working to attain, a brief explanation describing why you are involved in this campaign, and how to donate. If you have opened a campaign bank account, remember to include to who the check is payable, and where to send the check. Below is a template fundraising letter to assist you.

Fundraising Letter

February 5, 2020

Donna Bowen
812 Old Road Dr.
Anywhere, USA

Aunt Donna;

As you are aware, I am attending Western College and I am currently enjoying a wonderful senior year. After thorough consideration, I am excited to tell you that I have decided to run for the office of student body president at Western! In order to run for office, I will need to raise $500 in order to pay for my campaign. This will pay for campaign signs, fliers, and other materials needed to get my message out to voters.

Any help you can provide would be greatly appreciated. If you are able to donate to my campaign, please make a check or money order payable to "Campaign to Elect Jason Morton Western President" and mail it to the address on the envelope. You can also go to my website and make an online donation at www.JMorton4President.com.

Thank you for all of your love and support.

Sincerely,

Jason Morton

Jason Morton

Candidate for Student Body President

Western College

In addition to reaching out to family and friends, consider other traditional fundraising methods. You can raise money by hosting a bake sale, or hosting a party where admission fees benefit your campaign. If you can be creative and resourceful, your options are endless. Whatever fundraising method you choose, remember that it will reflect the campaign and the candidate running for office. If a fundraising event contradicts the principles of the campaign and portrays a negative campaign image, the event will only damage the campaign.

Many candidates belong to at least one student organization. These organizations take pride in their members excelling in leadership positions, and may be willing to lend a helping hand in your fundraising. Core staffers should consult the leadership from the organizations they belong to, and ask for financial support. If the organization is not willing to help you financially, be sure to thank them for their time regardless. You will need the support of this organization for votes, and a negative reaction to their inability to help you financially could leave a bad taste in their mouths.

Organizational financing should only be considered if all other options have failed. There could be an appearance of impropriety when accepting campaign dollars from outside organizations. It could appear to voters that when an organization pays you, it will want something in return if you win. This practice could also send a message to organizations that you are willing to provide political favors, even if you never made any such promise and have no intent to do so.

Good record keeping is a theme you will notice throughout this book. This is especially the case for fundraising. The first step in good fundraising records is to open a bank account. Bank records are meticulous, rarely incorrect, and are usually available anytime online. If for any reason campaign funds are not used for the campaign, it should be returned to the donor immediately. This is impossible if you are not effectively tracking where each and every dollar originated. There may also be campaign rules for disclosure of campaign finance records. This may include money coming in to the campaign as well as funds being spent.

Campaigns cost money, and you need it to run for office. You should understand your school's election by-laws which govern fundraising. Once you now the rules, there are several ways to raise the money; yet, it is imperative that you do so with caution. Poorly planned events could reflect poorly on a campaign. And a lack of good record keeping could even bring your entire campaign down before you even get started. If done correctly, you will have all of the financing you need to begin targeting voters with your campaign message.

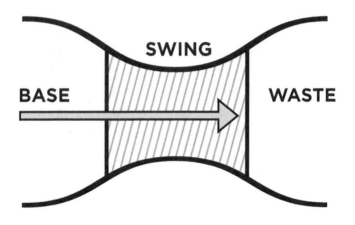

Chapter 6 — Base vs. Waste

Earlier, you assessed the demographics of your electorate and identified specific voting groups. Reaching out to each and every group would require unlimited funding, staff, and time. Here, you and your core staff will study the demographics to target the groups most suitable for your campaign.

Former U.S. House Majority Leader Dick Armey once said, "The first rule of politics is: don't lose the friends you already have for the friends you're never going to get." Put simply, the Representative was saying that when you reach out to voter groups who strongly oppose you, you risk losing the groups who support you. Certain groups with whom you have identified will have a natural draw to your campaign. Others, however, will not and may even be drawn away from you and to your opponent.

Before evaluating how each group will lean in your election, the size of the group should be measured. You may identify several groups who you are confident will be leaning heavily toward your candidacy, but if there are only a few voters in each of these groups, your research could mislead you. Evaluating the size of voting groups is not always a science and will require a good deal of estimation, depending on the quality of your earlier research. The more precise your data, the less you have to estimate. List each voting group and beside their name, and list how many voters you believe are in that group. Now that you are comfortable with the size of each of these voting groups, it is time to evaluate how each group may vote. Every single voting group that you have identified will fall in one of three categories of voter groups: Base, Waste, or Swing.

BASE

Merriam-Webster defines base as "the bottom of something considered as its support." Your campaign base voters are those people or groups who make up the foundation of your voting support. These people serve as the roots of your campaign's philosophy, principles, and ideals. These are groups who are close to your campaign either because you or those you have selected on your core team are members of those groups, or for some reason you have a close affiliation with them. Your base will not only vote for you, but they will organize for your campaign, and help you find others to support your campaign because you share the same principles and ideals as they do. Base groups support you because you are either one of them, or you unequivocally stand for the same things they stand for.

The novice campaigner has a strong tendency to subscribe to a blasé approach when selecting who his or her base voters are. This mistake could be the difference between winning and losing. Be very vigilant in this process, because if your campaign is built on an unstable foundation, it will crumble when you reach out to voters who may not agree with every single issue of your base. When your base is true and the connection to your campaign is strong, you will be able to reach out to more diverse voters while still enjoying the commitment and unwavering support of your base.

A few factors should be satisfied when making this decision. Are you or a member of your core team a member of this group? If so, is this person a committed member or just a member in name only (MINO)? For instance, did this person recently join the group in order to get their support for the election? If so, this person may not have earned the credibility necessary to call this group your base. In the occasion that none of your core members are part of the group you are assessing, you have to ask: What is the connection? Do you or someone in the campaign have a strong bond with a leader of the group or organization? And does this leader have the ability to convince the entire group to give its steadfast support? If these answers are not initially clear, these are probably not base organizations.

Example: Tracy is running for class president. Cameron is Tracy's selection for vice-president. Cameron is a popular student, a current student senator, and a new member of the school's marching band. Cameron assured Tracy that she could count on the support of the band, and Tracy designated the large band as a base group. Cameron recently joined the large band in hopes of securing the coveted "band vote." The only problem is, Cameron isn't really interested in music and doesn't even play an instrument! Other more dedicated band members can see through Cameron's transparent agenda, and have no plans in supporting him the upcoming elections.

Tracy's mistake of accepting, on its face, that the school band would be a base supporter of her campaign could have been avoided. By asking some simple follow-up questions to Cameron, Tracy could have recognized that the band was not a base group, but a group the campaign could progressively reach out to for support. By designating the band as a base group, she is placing the hopes of her campaign on commitment that simply does not exist.

Example: Jenny is running for student office. Her finance direc-tor, Joe, is an active member of a school community service organi-zation. Joe joined the organization during his freshman year, and has coordinated and managed several community service events. Joe has served as the group's recruitment director for three straight semes-ters, and has developed strong relationships with most of the group's members. Jenny acquires all of this information from asking Joe the appropriate questions. Additionally, she followed this up with a lunch meeting with the organization's President, who gave Joe a glowing assessment and even offered his group's support to Joe and Jenny's campaign efforts. Because Jenny performed her due dili-gence, she can safely designate the community service organization as a base voter group.

Later in the book, we will visit the topic of mobiliza-tion of voters. Simply put, there are two fundamental parts to winning votes. First, you must earn voter support and willingness to cast a vote for you. Second, students have to actually go to the polls and place a vote for you. It is not enough for voters to pledge their support for you, if they do not take the steps to actually vote for you. The process of classifying your base voting groups should always consider the factor of mobilization.

Example: Pedro is running for class president of his com-munity college. Pedro is a non-traditional student. He is twen-ty-nine years of age, and spent four years in the Navy be-fore attending college on the G.I. Bill. A large portion of the enrollment at the community college attends college on the G.I. Bill, and Pedro has gotten the committed support of many of his fellow veteran classmates. The majority of these non-traditional students, however, are not required to take classes on campus, and many only take online courses. Elections are held on one day only, and are held on-campus. Pedro had not considered this mobilization obstacle, and his candidacy relied heavily on the support and votes of military-veteran students. Since most of this voting group is not required to physically attend campus, they were unable to provide much help to Pedro's campaign. And since they will have to make a special trip to campus just to vote, many will not make it out to vote for Pedro.

Pedro may be able to overcome this mobilization problem by making arrangements for students to come to campus to vote. A carefully orchestrated voter transportation effort could get Pedro's supporters to the poles and lead him to victory. Nonetheless, this would have to be a consideration when deciding if this pool of voters should be a base voter group. And even if Pedro is able to get these voters to campus on election day, how will they provide the campaign support required by base voter groups? Whether or not this effort and time consumption is worthwhile should be discussed at this point in the campaign.

Base voters are essential and should never be taken for granted. If base voters are not repeatedly reminded why they should support and vote for you, you run the risk that they will lose the motivation to support you; or worse, vote for your opponent. "Cage rattling" is a phrase used to refer to the act of motivating your base by reminding them why you are the best candidate, and why your competitor is not.

Example: The basketball team is part of your base electorate. Your challenger just made a comment in the school paper that too many of the school's resources have been put towards athletics. He says that some sports should be cut in order free up resources for other programs. You react by attending a basketball meeting with copies of the newspaper clipping, and a warning that if the opponent is elected, their program may be in jeopardy.

WASTE

Waste voters are the opposite of base voters. These are voters who will most likely not be voting for you for one reason or another. This could be because your candidacy simply does not appeal to them, or it is because these groups are part of your competitor's base. Either way, courting these voters is not worth your campaign's resources. These resources should be spent solidifying your base, and reaching out to unaffiliated swing voters to possibly bring into your base.

As an aspiring politician, it is normal to want all voters to like you and your candidacy. It is tempting to want to speak to every organization in order to show that you are a reasonable person and a candidate with good intentions. Despite these tendencies, it is important to keep in mind that you do not need the support of every voter, just more than your competitor(s). These voters are designated as "waste" because it is a waste of your valuable time and resources to try to appeal to them.

Another potential problem with courting waste voters is that, in doing so, you could marginalize your base voters. Base voters are your foundation and they provide not only votes, but campaign support. There is no pay-off for trading a valuable base supporter for waste votes.

Example: At Valley Tech University, Pam is running for student body president. Pam's vice-president candidate, Landon, is a member of the Alpha Beta social fraternity, where he was recently president. Pam's competitor, Nate, is a member of Delta Gamma fraternity, the only other fraternity on campus and the arch rival of Alpha Beta. The brothers of Delta Gamma are in full support of Nate and are helping with his campaign. Pam, however, wanted a chance to convince Delta Gamma that she is a better choice than Nate and does so by meeting with them while taking several of their members to lunch. When the brothers of Alpha Beta see Pam going in and out of the Delta house and courting their leaders in the cafeteria, they begin to question her commitment to Alpha Beta. Soon, other brothers hear about this, and Pam's support from Alpha Beta begins to weaken.

SWING

The next category of voters to discuss is swing voters. You have likely heard this phrase before during national presidential elections. These voters usually have no determinable ties to either candidate and could "swing" to either side. These groups are neither a base group for you nor your opponent, and they are there for the taking. When both or all candidates have a secure base, swing voters will likely decide the election. The candidate, who is able to reach out and appeal to these voters, while maintaining and mobilizing his or her base voters, will win the election.

In order to fully understand what groups fall into the swing voter category, you should have a good idea of who your competitor(s) will be in the election. It is possible that at this point, you do not know exactly who your competition will be. If you have a good pulse on the organization for which you are running, however, you should at least have an idea of who is considering a run. Assess the field to find who your competitors will be. This will require you and your core team keeping an ear to the ground, and not being afraid to ask other students who have aspirations to run for office. If an opposing candidate is diligent, he/she will be active, and this will give you the hot trail you need to identify the opposition.

SCORING

In order to properly classify each identified voting group, it is very important to implement a scoring system. This will allow you to see where each group sits on the axis, and will illustrate to you which groups make up your base, which groups are a waste of time to try to connect, and which groups are within reach. By failing to appropriately align voting groups, you risk improperly depending on groups as your base, unnecessarily dismissing possible voters as waste, and confusion as to what voters to target in your campaign. Scoring is very important, and this section gives you step-by-step directions.

Three areas should be considered when scoring voting groups: size, support, and mobilization.

Size — A candidate could have a very large number of groups make up a base, yet if each group only has five students, the candidate needs to know this in order to find votes elsewhere. The size of a voting group can be easy discoverable if the group is a recognized student organization. Often times, however, you will have identified groups which are not recognized student organizations at the school and acquiring information on these groups require you to make an educated guess. This process will require your team to be as creative and precise as possible.

Example: Janet is running for class president. Of the 48 student groups she has identified, one of the groups is made up of commuter students who ride their bikes to school. Janet has checked with the Dean of Students and the director of public safety, but unfortunately, there are no records that reflect the size of this student population. As a result, Janet worked with the director of public safety to find out exactly where each bike rack is located on campus, and she sent campaign workers to each rack to count the bikes during the busiest times of the week. This information provided Janet and her team the information she needed to make an educated guess about the number of commuter bikers at her school.

When making a size determination, remember that students are often parts of multiple voting groups. For instance, while Juanita is a commuter who rides her bike to class, she is also part of a local sorority. If this consideration is not made, your numbers will be inflated and you risk depending on two votes when you actually only have one.

Support — The next important factor to consider is support level. This score will determine whether the group is a base, waste, or swing group. Making this assessment is often subjective, but should be made by your core team by considering several factors. First, consider what incentive there is for each group to vote for you or your candidate and the other candidate(s). How does the candidate assist this group in their mission? Next, consider what affiliations your team has to a particular group. Are there members of your core team who are members of this organization? If so, are they respected members who possess legitimate influence on these students? Also consider if your core members have close friends or family members who are part of these organizations. It is also essential to consider if your opponent has connections, affiliations, or relationships with these groups, because this will affect their support for you.

Mobilization — In addition to size and support, a candidate must always consider mobilization. As previously mentioned, the size and support level of a group means nothing if that group will not go to the polls on election day and actually cast a vote for you. See Pedro example. When scoring a group for mobilization, first consider how convenient it is for this group to vote for you. Consider where the polls are and how accessible the voting will be. Next, consider whether this group is internally structured. Organized groups communicate regularly, and if the organization supports you, they are more likely to keep one another informed as to when, where, and how to vote. Alternatively, rogue groups have no central organization to keep one another informed; thus the chances of them mobilizing to the polls will decrease. Lastly, remember that support and mobilization are not mutually exclusive. The level of support a group has will usually correlate with the chances of them voting for you because they have more motivation to go to the polls; nevertheless, a candidate should consider convenience and the level of the group's internal organization to make a valid determination.

Now that you know who the groups are and what the appropriate metrics are in scoring them, it is time to put numbers on each group. There are a number of ways to organize the scoring procedure, but the suggested method is assigning each organization an index card. On each index card write the name of the organization on top in big letters. Next make a place for support, size, and mobilization scores. Use a pencil so that you can make changes. You can use the back of the card to make any necessary notes to remember about each organization during discussions.

Assessments of each group and scoring should be done with your core team so that you get several perspectives. The campaign manager should facilitate the discussion with the core team by reviewing each voting group individually. In order to avoid letting this process go on for too long, it

Sample Organization Index Card

Group Name: Ladies Basketball Team **B**
Support Score: 9.5
Size Determination: 12 voters
Mobilization Score: 5

Notes: The team is very supportive since our candidate is a former trainer for the team and has a personal relationship with almost all of the girls on the team.

The team has an away game scheduled during voting week; however they are scheduled to be back to campus by the second (last) day of voting. Plans will need made to mobilize the entire team on the last day of elections.

Group Name: College Republicans **W**
Support Score: 2
Size Determination: 30 voters
Mobilization Score: 10

Notes: The College Republicans will likely support Chet Broward who is a former College Republican president who is running against us. We do have a connection: Our press secretary is dating a new member of the CR's. This will likely not overcome Chet's support.

is important to limit the discussion for each group to a certain time limit. This is especially true if you have identified several groups.

Each voting group will be assigned a support score, a size determination, and a mobilization score. The scale for the support score and the mobilization score are one through ten. Fractions should be used for more specific determinations. Use the factors and considerations mentioned above. In regards to size, be as specific as you can and remember to be creative when you are unable to be specific.

After thorough discussion(s) among you and your team, you should have a completed group index card reflecting a support score, size determination, and mobilization score for each voting group. The next step is to display all of the cards on the axis. It is suggested that you do this by taping group index cards on a large wall so that your group can see all of the cards. Placement is based solely on support scores, so ignore size and mobilization scores during this step. You will put the card with the highest support score the furthest to the left. As the support scores increase, place the cards up until the lowest score is placed furthest to the right side.

When you have each group properly placed on the voter axis, you are ready to assess your base. Groups who have been assigned a support score of eight or higher will be your base voter groups. The cards which make up your base should be distinguished in some way, so that the team gets a clear picture of what groups make up the base. This can be done by putting a large "B" on these cards, by color coding them with a highlighter, or by drawing a line perpendicular to the horizontal axis after the card of the last base group. After you have prominently distinguished who the base groups are, add up all of the sizes of each support group.

Once you have a total number of voters who make up your base, you will factor in your support score and mobilization scores.

Organization Axis

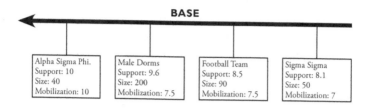

BASE

Alpha Sigma Phi.
Support: 10
Size: 40
Mobilization: 10

Male Dorms
Support: 9.6
Size: 200
Mobilization: 7.5

Football Team
Support: 8.5
Size: 90
Mobilization: 7.5

Sigma Sigma
Support: 8.1
Size: 50
Mobilization: 7

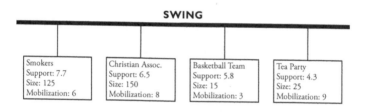

SWING

Smokers
Support: 7.7
Size: 125
Mobilization: 6

Christian Assoc.
Support: 6.5
Size: 150
Mobilization: 8

Basketball Team
Support: 5.8
Size: 15
Mobilization: 3

Tea Party
Support: 4.3
Size: 25
Mobilization: 9

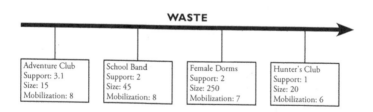

WASTE

Adventure Club
Support: 3.1
Size: 15
Mobilization: 8

School Band
Support: 2
Size: 45
Mobilization: 8

Female Dorms
Support: 2
Size: 250
Mobilization: 7

Hunter's Club
Support: 1
Size: 20
Mobilization: 6

Unless all of your support and mobilization scores are perfect tens, you will have to make deductions to account for the scores. First, get an average support score for all of your base groups. This is done by adding the scores and dividing by the number of base groups. Once you have the average support score, you turn this score into a whole number by moving the decimal over one position to the right. If there is no fraction, just add a zero to the score. This will give you a two digit number that becomes the percentage of voters which will support you. To get a raw number of voters, multiply the number of base voters by the percentage.

Next, you have to account for the mobilization scores that were assigned to each group. This process is the same as before. Determine an average mobilization score for each base group. Once this number is determined, move the decimal over one position to the right. If there is no fraction, add a zero. This new number is the percentage of supporters that you feel will actually go to the polls and cast a vote for your candidate. Now take the new raw number, determined by factoring in support scores, and find the new percentage by multiplying the new number by the mobilization percentage. This new number reflects your total number of base voters.

It is also very important to consider that many voters will fall in multiple groups, and have been counted multiple times depending on how many groups they are a member. For example, Pamela may be in three of your recognized groups: Commuter sorority girls, The College Democrat Club, and the Woman's Rights Club. Your calculations may depend on Pamela's vote three different times if each of these groups are in your base. In order to account for this problem, deduct another four percent from the final number of base voters you have determined. This will take a step towards avoiding inflated base numbers.

Remember, this is not a scientific number, but one that will give you an idea of what direction your campaign should go in order to secure the votes needed to win the election. To put things in further prospective with your team; add up the total number of voters you have identified through voter groups, and then calculate the percentage of those total voters that are made up by base voters. This should illustrate to your team that there is a lot of work to be done to gather the votes needed to win half plus one.

The next step is to make the same determination with your waste voter groups. A waste organization is any organization in which you gave a support score of three or lower. First, you want to get a total number by adding up all of the sizes of the waste groups. Then, you account for the support scores by getting an average support score and then deducting that percentage from the original number. This gives you a lower total number of waste voters.

The next step is accounting for mobilization. Like before, determine an average mobilization score of each waste group. Next, turn that number into a percentage and then deduct that percentage from the new total number, once you accounted for support level. Since it is possible that there is a crossover of voter group members, deduct another four percent. You should now have the total number of voters for which you should not spend one campaign resource chasing during your campaign.

Campaign Spending

Sample Spreadsheet Graphic

ITEM	COST	LOCATION	NOTES	DEDUCTED FROM LIMIT (500.00)
Plywood	$150.00	Lumber Depot	For Campaign Signs	$350.00
Ink	$50.00	Ink Inc.	For fliers and brochures	$300.00
Paper	$20.00	Paper Outlet	For fliers and brochures and other administrative campaign uses	$280.00
Paint	$50.00	Paint R Us	Campaign signs	$230.00
Sidewalk chalk	$20.00	School Supply Mart	Sidewalk art near cafeteria	$210.00
Drinking water	$25.00	Dollar Mart	For team campaigning on campus	$185.00
Clip boards	$20.00	School Supply Mart	For campaign team around campus	$165.00
Website domain	$15.00	Domains. com	For campaign website hosting	$150.00

The next assessment explores a group of voters who you certainly do want to spend time appealing to. These are the swing voters, and these are groups who you assigned a support score between three and eight. Nonetheless, we are going to split them into two classes. First is Swing A, which are the groups with support scores between three and five. Swing B, who will be tougher to attract, are the groups with support scores between five and eight. Swing groups make up the middle of your axis, and you should draw a line between Swing A and B to make it clear to your team. It is imperative that you get to know as much as possible about your swing voters, because most of your campaign will be designed to reach out to these voters while keeping a firm hold on your base.

Just like before, we need to determine how many vot-ers exist with these classes. First, take Swing A and add up the total amount of voters. Make the proper deductions by determining a percentage for support scores and mobilization scores. Deduct another four percent to account for the possible crossover of members. Do the exact same thing for Swing B voting groups so that you have a total number of voters for each swing group.

Implementing a proper scoring plan and taking the necessary time to execute it with your team will allow you to identify the voters needed to win your election. The process allows you to use all of the information you have accumulated so that you can cater to your base, evade your waste, and reach for those swing voters who have no ties or affiliation with either candidate. This is done by crafting a campaign platform that appeals to the voters you need, while solidifying the voters you already have. It is also done by assembling a complete staff who can help reach out to those much needed voter groups for support.

Calculating Vote Count

SWING A

Total Voters:	130
Average Support Score:	7
	130 x .70 = 91
Average Mobilization Score:	8.3
	91 x .83 = 75.5
Total SWING A Vote Count:	75

SWING B

Total Voters:	220
Average Support Score:	5.5
	220 x .55 = 121
Average Mobilization Score:	6.5
	121 x .65 = 78.65
Total SWING B Vote Count:	78

Complete Staff Checklist:

✓ *Campaign Manager*
✓ *Vice President or running mate (if needed)*
✓ *Finance Director (Treasure)*

✓ *Press Secretary (Public Relations)*
✓ *Graphics Coordinator*
✓ *Digital Director*
✓ *Advertising Director*
✓ *Constituency Liaisons*

Chapter 7 — Assembling a Complete Team

According to an old English proverb, "A man is only as good as the company he keeps." Each staff member should be competent in their respective area, and a good ambassador to the student body. A great staff can help neutralize any shortcomings of the candidate by perfecting all important areas of a successful campaign. And no matter what position a staffer holds, he/she is an ambassador for the candidate. If a voter does not personally know the candidate, they will deferto one of the campaign's staffers to judge the credibility of the campaign.

Besides being an ambassador for you, it is important that each member of your staff be capable of managing at least one aspect of your campaign from day one. Like all other phases of your campaign, you must consider maximizing your vote when assembling a staff. Nonetheless, a balancing test should be administered so that competency is not severely compromised. If an ineffectual staff is assembled, your campaign will lose efficiency and is likely be unsuccessful. Thus, finding a good balance between competence and your particular demographic need is critical. By merely selecting students who are popular, you take an unnecessary risk. This risk can be avoided by you and your core staff by taking the time to find those students who are effective diplomats, and are competent to accomplish the important goals you set out for them.

> **Example:** Bill is running for student body president. He already has his core staff in order and he is now in the process of choosing a press secretary. One of the groups making up the swing vote in Bill's campaign is the coveted Marching Band, made up of 140 members. Jessica is a senior flute player in the band, and currently serves as vice-president of the Marching Band. She has been in the band since she was a freshman and is on a first name basis with all its members. Jessica majors in music with a minor in sculpting, and has no experience in journalism, public relations, or campaigns of any kind. In spite of her lack of experience, Bill decides to hire Jessica as his press secretary with hopes of securing the valuable band vote. Instead, Jessica struggles with adapting with the new job and her duties with the band. Confused and unable to keep up, Jessica resigns from the campaign with two weeks remaining, leaving Bill without a press secretary.

Bill hired Jessica as press secretary despite her inexperience. The job of press secretary requires skills which are often too complex to acquire in the midst of a fast moving campaign. Instead, Bill could have appointed Jessica the liaison to the Marching Band, and her duties would have been drastically minimized while she was part of the campaign.

At this point, you should already have the core positions of vice-president (if required), campaign manager, and finance director. For some campaigns, this may be all you need to continue. The office for which you are running will dictate your need and what kind of staff members you will require. Even if you may not completely need more positions, it may be beneficiary to provide titles with responsibilities to those who are committed to your campaign. Volunteers appreciate titles because it shows they are formally included and it provides some reward for a job with no financial compensation. It also shows voters that you have a formal team in place, and that you are capable of managing them.

Below is a list of positions you should consider filling for your campaign. Beside each position is a brief description to help explain how this person will contribute to your campaign. The importance of these positions will depend on your particular campaign.

Press Secretary (Also known as Director of Public Relations)
This can be a demanding position which requires a high level of competency. The press secretary is responsible for making sure the campaign is getting positive press coverage in the media as often as possible. This requires the ability to prepare press releases, issue statements on behalf of the campaign, and preferably have numerous contacts within media outlets covering the campaign in order to convey a positive image of your campaign. If there are no media outlets available at your school, the press secretary must be creative in finding other ways to shine a positive light on your candidacy throughout the campaign.

Graphics Coordinator

A graphics coordinator is responsible for designing all campaign logos and literature. Most voters will remember your campaign only through its advertising efforts, so the creation of this identity is crucial to the success of the campaign. This is another position which demands a competent person with the necessary graphic design skills.

Digital Director

In today's age, a campaign for a campus-wide office should have its own website. The web page will provide the voters with in-depth information to be reviewed on the voters' own time. It is important to have a professional website that reflects the qualities of your campaign. In order to do this, a good digital director must be chosen to take on the task of creating and maintaining the site throughout the campaign. The digital director should also maintain a strong identity on social networking sites like Facebook, Twitter, and Instagram. As new networking sites and applications inevitably become available, the digital director must stay up to date with the popular outlets students are using.

Advertising Director

Sign-making is a very important part of campaigns. It gives the candidate name recognition to the average student walking through campus. Some students decide to have signs professionally made, but with spending limits and low college income, this is often difficult. The advertising director will be responsible for the campaign's signs. This includes what they look like, where they are placed, when and where the staff will work on them, etc. This is a big undertaking that will be physically demanding and time consuming. It is preferable to have someone who is creative, artistic, and has experience in advertising. It is also nice if they own a truck!

Constituency Liaisons (to any target group)

In order to bridge the gap to the groups who make up the swing voters, you can appoint liaisons from those groups. For example, if you are shooting for the ROTC vote, you may appoint a liaison to military students or the ROTC. This person should be popular within the ROTC and preferably is respected by its members. This liaison is responsible for educating the ROTC about the campaign, setting up speaking engagements for the candidate with the ROTC, and mobilizing all of the members on election day to get out and vote. You can have liaisons for any and all groups who make up your swing voters. These positions are very important in keeping your ear to the ground as to the needs of your target groups, getting you in the door to speak with them at their meetings, and mobilizing target groups to vote on election day.

Assembling a staff is different for everyone. It depends on your need. Be strategic and balance bringing in students from target groups with acquiring the competency needed to run a complex campaign. Compromising the skills needed for multifaceted positions is often counter-productive. Remember, you are free to create positions for those who do not fit the mold for other, more demanding jobs. All the groups identified as target groups, and lie in the swing voter area of your spectrum, should have a liaison appointed from within the groups in order to bridge the gap with those high-valued groups and mobilize voters.

Chapter 8 — Image

An image is an idea that someone has about someone, and to a political candidate, it is everything. Your image is shaped, almost exclusively, by you and your team. Although there are other influences that affect your image, the way you and your team carry yourselves will be the predominant driver to how people see you and your campaign.

The first step in creating and maintaining a positive image is to be aware that everything you do will be more scrutinized once you decide to run for office. This elevated scrutiny is not limited to the time you are acting in a political capacity; but will expand into your personal life. Seasoned candidates are aware that people are continuously watching and paying attention to how they handle every situation, in order to expediently create an image of the candidate. This new social analysis, although at a less elevated level, extends to your campaign team members as well. If you and your team are always aware of this new social responsibility, it is less likely that there will be any issues.

In addition to making your team aware of the elevated scrutiny of their actions, candidates and campaign managers should also consider implementing guidelines or rules for the team. For less mature team members, these guidelines will be easier to follow because they are unequivocal. Whatever guidelines established, it is very important that the candidate and the officers of the campaign also strictly follow them, and not just low level volunteers.

Example: Francis is running for class president at Duncan University, and she has a core team of five staffers and another twenty volunteers since the school is relatively large. Several of Francis' volunteers are members of the Greek community and frequently attend parties, and recently have used these outings to spread their candidate's message. In order to avoid any foreseeable problems, Francis' campaign manager implemented a "no drinking" rule for campaign workers while at parties. With this rule, there is no chance that the volunteers will have too much to drink, which often leads to making poor decisions. Additionally, the campaign manager implemented a curfew mandating that volunteers had to leave parties by 11:00 P.M. sharp.

For any candidate, it is very important to meet people and to be seen in a positive light. For those running at the college level, being seen often requires the candidate's participation in student nightlife. College students spend lots of their free time blowing off steam and enjoying their new found freedom. For a candidate, nightlife can present a difficult balance. It is important to appear social and "in touch" with mainstream life, yet the candidate also needs to appear credible and professional at all times.

There are a few rules to consider when the candidate is participating in those social gatherings: 1) Use good judgment in deciding what functions to attend. When binge drinking is foreseeable, you can usually predict that something unexpected may happen, so you should always avoid these situations. Attending these events say that you endorse this behavior and this will alienate you from a large portion of voters. 2) Arrive fashionably late and leave responsibly early. This will reduce the amount of time you spend there and will give more value to the time spent. It will also limit the possibility of anything bad happening. 3) If you are of age and you must partake in alcoholic drinks, limit yourself to just one drink. This is enough to show that you are "in touch," which is the only reason you should be partaking at all. 4) Lastly, go to the party or event with someone who is sure to know people in attendance, so that you can be properly introduced. Going to party and not knowing anyone will force you to introduce yourself to everyone. This may give the appearance of politicking, which may seem disingenuous considering the environment.

As mentioned earlier, there is a heightened scrutiny applied to those running for political office, and this scrutiny often extends to the candidate's personal life. Parents often tell their kids they are only as good as the company they keep. This does not just go for your campaign team, but also the company you keep in your personal time. If a candidate is seen socializing with certain people, it is likely that the candidate's image will be linked to those people. If there are polarizing figures in a candidate's life, it may be worth creating some space from those figures while you are running a campaign. Understandably, some candidates refuse to do this because of their loyalty to friends or family. If this is the case, be aware that you will likely be judged on how your close friends conduct themselves, regardless of your participation in the act.

Another way to portray a positive image to voters is by participating in community service. Nothing reveals someone's compassion like helping others. By working on a community service project with student organizations, you can show you are willing to help others. It also allows you to showcase the leadership skills needed to be a student leader. If this is the only time you have ever done community service and you are not subtle in your approach to marketing it, community service will appear spurious and disingenuous. Work closely with your public relations director to ensure this is handled properly.

> **Example:** Michael is running for senior class president at his small college. During his freshman year, he joined a community service organization and volunteered a total of twenty-five hours his first year. During his sophomore and junior year, Michael didn't answer the calls of the organization and he did not volunteer. Now in his senior year and running for class president, Michael begins volunteering actively. Although appreciative of the help, Michael's fellow organization members realize that his new found sense of public service is motivated by his campaign. Word spreads fast that Michael's own organization members are unhappy with him, and vow not to vote for him. This severely damages Michael's image with his organization and other voters who have become aware of Michael's insincerity.

Chapter 9 — Platform Design & Strategic Plan

A platform is your campaign's proposed agenda to the voters. A good campaign platform will focus on only a handful of core areas. By making these platform areas broad, you can fit many different issues under each area. The idea is that you advertise the principles you will govern by, and leave the specific policies for those interested in reading further into your campaign. Policies can be mind-numbing and will not capture the attention of the average voter. Unless there is one controlling issue on campus that requires you to prominently display your position, it would be wise to bullet-point your guiding principles and give the voters the choice to look more closely.

At this point, you should already have your finger on the pulse of your electorate from your discussions with student leaders and conversations with various voters. You and your team should have a solid understanding of the issues that affect your school and where you stand on those issues. This section provides some assistance on how to choose what issues you plan to address, and how to package those positions so that it can be easily articulated to the voters.

Example: Tyrel is running for student office, and his base groups consist of Alpha Beta fraternity and the basketball team. By speaking with members of each group, he was informed as to the major concerns of each. AB fraternity is concerned that the school doesn't do enough to provide cheap entertainment to students while on campus. The basketball players would like to see an increase in students at the basketball games, in order to create a more difficult environment for opponents and added motivation for the home team. With this information, Tyrel makes it a campaign platform goal to provide affordable seating and a fun environment at athletic events. He promises to focus his efforts on making athletic events fun and easily accessible for students. It is likely that this proposal will be appealing to other groups of students as well, without the chance of offending his base. This leaves other core issues of his platform to focus more towards swing voters.

It is always necessary to consider what the popular issues and positions are among your voters. The harsh reality is that this campaign is not about you; it is about the students, and regardless of how passionate you are about an issue, it must be something that will get voters' attention and get them to the polls to vote for your campaign. It is, however, helpful if you are passionate about issues because it conveys that you are genuine and that you have a firm understanding of the issues. Regardless of your personal feelings, the issues of your platform must be ones that get voters to the polls because it affects them.

Example: Daniel is a student at Fairfax High, and he lives in an area called Hill Crest in which the school bus does not run. Because of this, Daniel and four other students are forced to walk two miles each morning to get to a bus stop in the next town. While making this long trek each morning, the four students complain that something needs to be done to fix this, and one of the walkers suggests that Daniel run for junior class president in order to persuade the school to require the bus to come closer to their neighborhood. Daniel agrees, runs for the position, and makes a campaign promise that he will fight for a bus that will come to Hill Crest and pick up students. This promise turned out to be highly effective among the four students who wanted the bus; however, this issue did nothing to motivate the majority of voters to vote for Daniel.

There are a few things Daniel could have done to be more successful in drafting his campaign platform. First, he should have considered how his Hill Crest bus issue would play with voters. Although he clearly had a passion for the issue, it was not an issue that mattered to the majority of his voters. Instead of dropping the issue altogether, Daniel could have considered broadening the discussion so that it would relate to a larger number of students. For example, Daniel could have campaigned on expanding bus routes for all students. If other students in different neighborhoods are being forced to walk because buses do not reach their neighborhoods, this issue may resonate with more students.

Previously, we studied base versus waste voters, and identified who were the base, waste, and swing voters. When deciding what issues to focus your campaign on, remember that you have two main groups to consider. Base voters cannot be taken for granted, and although they may be your biggest advocates now, it is possible that you lose them if you do not include their key issues in your platform. Second, you have to reach out to swing voters by including issues that speak to those groups. Issues that resonate predominately with groups which fall under waste groups should simply be avoided and left to your competitors to address.

The more complicated you make your platform on its face, the less interested the common voter will be in your campaign. Young people today possess shortened attention spans, thanks in part to the increased amount of information we receive at once. When trying to get the attention of your audience, you are often competing with thousands of other sources of information; thus, your message must be quick, creative, and effective. How is your message going to make a lasting impression when thousands of other messages have been hurled at them on the same day? Be quick, creative, and effective.

Unless there is a hot-button issue on campus, single issues or positions rarely get voters' attention because it may not relate to a large number of voters. If, however, you portray the general principles of your campaign, a larger number of students may become interested and look further for more detail on your campaign. Students may not care so much about Daniel's position on getting a bus to Hill Crest, but if he advertised to students that he stood for better bus routes, a larger number of students may relate.

Example: Heidi is running for student body president at State College. She has identified a number of popular issues among students including the lack of dormitory parking, malfunctioning elevators in the History Building, and no online registration for summer classes. Instead of listing these issues on the front of her campaign material, Heidi instead advertises to students that her goal is to "Improve Student Convenience." When students look further into her campaign material, they see that she plans to improve dormitory parking, fix broken elevators in academic buildings, and work to create an online registration system for summer classes. Heidi can also add more items to this list if she feels there are additional issues she would like to address under "Convenience."

In a campus-wide election, platforms will be required to include multiple principles because of the diversity of issues facing the student body. If possible, it helps to be able to package these principles into something easy for voters to remember. This can be done using an acronym on a catchy slogan. For example, if you have five core principles, you could call your platform your "Strive for Five." Or you could use a star as your logo because it has five points. You can be creative in naming the pillars of your campaign so that you create a catchy acronym. For example, you can say your pillars are Convenience, Accessibility, and Recreation (C.A.R.). You could make your campaign logo a type of vehicle as a way to emphasize your platform. You could advertise your core principles as Convenience, Academics, Med School, and Universal Grading System so that the acronym is C.A.M.P.U.S. The possibilities are limitless if you and your team are creative.

Once you have identified the issues that will stimulate your base and reach out to swing voters, and you have packaged your agenda so that you are able to articulate the principles of your campaign; it is time to teach your team how to sell it. Members of your staff should be able to sum up your campaign in the time of a short elevator ride. Elevator rides usually last between one and two minutes, so this can be difficult. Your staff, however, should be able to summarize the platform's key points within this time so that the voter is able to get a broad understanding of why he/she should vote for you. The platform should not be memorized but internalized, meaning that the staff fully understands the principles and ideas behind the platform. The candidate should do what is needed to insure that all staff members have internalized the platform. If a staff member is not completely confident and sure about their explanation to a voter, the voter will immediately pick up on this and they too will be unsure of your message.

A platform is your campaign's proposed agenda to the voters. It communicates to the voter what you plan to do if you are elected to office. Unrealistic promises will likely be sniffed out by the voters, so keep goals attainable and simple to understand. Platforms should be packaged and marketed like a product because, simply put: a campaign is the art of selling a candidate to an electorate. The candidate is more marketable if the platform appeals to the target audience. Design your platform around the interests of your base voters, and those swing voters you plan to attain, in order to win the votes needed.

Chapter 10 — Endorsements

It can be beneficial for a candidate to secure the public endorsement of someone with influence over other potential voters. Political pundits often debate whether candidate endorsements are an effective use of campaign time. Critics suggest that people pay little attention to endorsements from individuals or organizations, but instead voters will use their own personal judgment to understand the positions of each candidate and then make a calculated decision. Others, including the author of this book, counter that many voters often trust the judgment of someone who has previously earned their confidence. Members of an organization may vote with the leadership of that organization, trusting the leadership in considering the well-being of its members.

The endorsements of organizational leaders on campus could lead to an entire group voting for your candidacy. If the leadership of an organization decides to endorse a candidate, the members will usually be asked by the organization leaders to place their vote for this candidate because that candidate will support their organization. And although members have the right to vote for whomever they choose, members will often take their leaders' advice and vote for the preferred candidate if they have no other prevailing reason to vote for someone else.

Candidates should focus on gaining endorsements from groups who make up base and swing groups in an effort to solidify the base and reach out to selected swing organizations.

It may not be possible to reach each and every student organization for their endorsement, so it is important to begin with your base groups and then move to your swing groups. Use the continuum from Chapter 6 to gauge which groups score the highest in order to prioritize speaking engagements. Once you have met with all of your base groups, begin meeting with swing groups. Do this as early as possible, because if the other candidate(s) beat you to the punch, these leaders may have already committed to your challenger(s) and you will be left fighting for other votes. Additionally, be careful with securing endorsements from controversial organizations.

Example: In her race for the student representative on the college's Honor Board, Tasha attempted to acquire organizational endorsements. One of Tasha's strongest base groups was the College Christian Society, who had 150 members and have endorsed Tasha's candidacy. Hungry for more endorsements, Tasha met with the campus Atheist Club, who has just thirteen members, and she gained their blessing. Both endorsements were advertised prominently on Tasha's literature, and the Christians became very upset with Tasha; and as a result, pulled their endorsement. In gaining the support of the Atheists, Tasha potentially lost several votes. Although it was tempting to gain as much support as possible, Tasha should have considered the consequences of reaching out to a group whose existence stirs deep emotions from other students. Tasha could have appealed to the Atheist Club, but it was very damaging for her to publicly display her affiliation with the group.

When making the hard ask to a campus leader, do it in person and not over phone, email, or any kind of electronic device. When a wedding proposal is made, it is done so in the most personal and persuasive way possible. Whoever is popping the question controls the circumstances in order to make it very difficult for their loved one to say no. The proposer controls the environment for the big question and exactly how the proposal will be framed. Usually the proposer gets on one knee, holds their loved one's hand, and looks directly into their eyes to ask for their hand in marriage. These conditions make it difficult to say no! You can control the environment in which you pop your question; and even though it is not recommended that you get down on one knee, it is important that you take this commitment very seriously and consider all of the details of how it is done.

For the base groups who score very high, it is essential that you meet with their leaders personally and ask them directly if they will endorse you. It is tempting to do this at a group meeting when you can address multiple officers; yet, the hard ask is much more effective when you have the undivided attention of the clubs top executive. In addition to making the hard ask, it is important to bring something to the table. Give the group leader a good reason to endorse you by clearly and succinctly explaining to this leader exactly how their group will benefit from you holding office. For example, if you are meeting with the leader of a community service organization, you may want to stress a particular point of your platform that will benefit them. If you make a hard and direct ask and give them a reason to endorse you, your chances of getting that endorsement are high. Even if you are not able to secure the endorsement, the worst thing they can say is "no."

Example: Tommy is student senator at his college. In his continuum which ranks organizations, it reflects that the community service fraternity on campus scores very high as his top base organization. It's a large group, and several of his close friends in the dorms are ranking members of the club. Since Tommy values this base group, he personally calls the president and asks him if he would like to meet for coffee on campus to discuss his candidacy. The president agrees and the two meet at Common Grounds, the school's coffee shop. After exchanging pleasant introductions, Tommy gets straight to the point and says, "I've asked you to meet because I'd like to ask for your support in my campaign for student senator." He continues, "If elected, I'd like to do a few things; one of which is to direct more school resources and time toward doing more service in the community, and we would follow the lead of your club in doing this." After hearing Tommy's short elevator speech, the president was inspired and agreed to endorse Tommy's run for student senate.

An endorsement from a club's top leader does not necessarily translate into an endorsement from the entire organization. Hopefully, the leader will influence his or her members to vote for you; however, it is not appropriate to claim that you have the endorsement of the entire organization unless that is what you are granted. It is a good idea to make these second hard asks after the representative gives you his or her blessing. If the organization's top officer grants the club's endorsement, you will have the green light to stake a claim to the endorsement. Some leaders, nonetheless, will want to talk it over with other leaders, or even put it to a vote before the entire membership. If this is the answer, make sure you inform the officer that you will get back to them very soon for the answer.

If you are unable to secure a one-on-one meeting with the top leader in each of these groups, settle for meeting them in a group setting. If you are unable to secure even that, attempt to get face-time with the vice-president or another ranking officer. The longer you wait to get some kind of leadership endorsement, the more chance you are giving your opponent(s) to come in and steal your endorsement. Just because you may consider this group your base does not mean that your opponent is writing it off as waste. There may be an unknown connection, and you have to strike first when it comes to your base.

Often, another member of your team will have an inside track with leaders of an organization in which you do not possess. When this is the case, it is important that you utilize this connection in order to gain the access needed to make the hard ask. Your campaign manager should reach out to everyone on your team to inquire if anyone has close ties to any organization, not just base and swing groups. This way, you and your manager can decide for yourselves if it is worth your time to meet with that group. Additionally, it may be a good idea to take your teammate, who has the access with that group, to the meeting with that group. This will make things more comfortable for everyone involved.

If your time is limited and you are unable to attend, consider sending a surrogate on your behalf. This could be your vice-presidential candidate, or another trusted advocate of your campaign who is prepared to make your pitch to student leaders. It is always preferred that you make the pitch yourself, since you are essentially asking these leaders to endorse your candidacy. And unless it is absolutely impossible for you to be present personally, it is better to send someone than no one at all. In the event that you must send a surrogate, it is imperative that the representative of your choice be someone who can properly embody your campaign and its message. This may require substantial preparation.

In addition to organization leaders, there may be other influential individuals on campus who you could consider asking for an endorsement. These may be students or former students who have held the office you are seeking. There is no better judge of whether you are qualified than someone who knows you and understands what it takes to be successful in the position for which you are seeking. This is especially true if the former officer is or was popular with other students. On the other hand, an unpopular or unsuccessful officer's public support of you could steer voters away from voting for you. It may also be helpful to seek out the support of other popular students on campus, such as athletes, whose opinion students may value. Remember, even though it is the voters' responsibility to educate themselves as to the candidates and their platforms, it rarely happens because 1) College students are very busy people who are juggling academics, extracurricular activities, and a need for social interaction, and 2) Students often see student office as unimportant and ineffective. As a result, student elections can sometimes turn into popularity contests. Since this is often the reality, especially at the middle and high school levels, it is important to personally reach out to as many voters as possible.

Getting endorsements are rarely useful unless you make other students aware that these individuals and groups vouch for your candidacy. There are a number of ways to flaunt your endorsements, and you should be resourceful in publicizing them. One way is to publish endorsements is in brochures or other types of literature. In order to accomplish this, it is necessary to give yourself a deadline to secure your endorsements so that you can include them in the design of your campaign literature. You can also post a list of endorsements on your website or on social networking sites.

Include the titles of those who are endorsing you, and the name of the organization for which they represent. If you gain the endorsement of an entire organization, include their logos on the list, so that readers will immediately recognize them without taking the time to read the text.

Another good method of using your endorsements is to ask individuals to write letters to the school newspaper. Good letters are like campaign advertisements. Letters allow voters to hear someone, outside of your campaign, sing your praises. They should be short and succinct, since readers will likely not take the time to read a long letter. Additionally, a shorter letter will make a bigger impact.

Sample Letter to the Editor

Letter to the Editor

Endorsement for Candy Date for President

I have had the pleasure of knowing Candy Date for the past three years as her residential advisor in Mars Hall. During this time, I have gotten to know Candy very well. She is hard working, genuine, and truly cares about our great university. These attributes would make Candy a fine president and that is why I proudly support her candidacy.

I will vote for Candy on Tuesday at the Memorial Student Center, and I ask that you do the same.

Sincerely,

Carolyn Newman

Carolyn Newman

Residential Advisor

Mars Hall

When asking for your advocates to write letters to the editor, urge them to send them near election day, if possible. If letters are published sooner, chances are that the voters will not remember. Bear in mind, however, that you may not be able to control when the letter is published; accordingly, candidates should insure the letters are submitted to the newspaper editor one week before the elections, and the press secretary should be sure to ask the editor to publish them on or near election day.

Endorsements can bring credibility to your campaign and can be very useful in influencing other students to vote for you. Students are too preoccupied with other aspects of life to become entrenched in campus politics, so sometimes it is just easier to trust someone else's opinion of a candidate. Yet students will never know of your endorsements unless you prominently display them for everyone to see. Elections are a game of thin margins, and your endorsements could mean the difference in your election.

Chapter 11 — Campaign Materials

Your campaign material will be the identity of your campaign to the majority of voters. Although it is ideal to personally meet every voter in order to make a positive impression, it is usually impractical. This is especially the case with campus-wide elections. Even if students have taken the time to meet the candidate, campaign materials serve as a reminder to vote for that candidate. Students who are not able to meet with the candidate will make both subtle and patent judgements based on materials distributed. These materials can include yard signs, brochures, fliers, and any other creative marketing tactic you employ. Materials should reflect the same qualities in which you try to express when you are personally speaking with voters, and they should also provide clear and succinct goals of the campaign.

Before you buy your materials and host sign making parties, you will need to craft a design for your campaign. As computers have become mainstream in our society, it is much easier to find a capable graphic designer at today's schools. If your school is fortunate enough to offer a program in graphic design, you can probably find a student to assist you in your design free of charge. These students are looking to broaden their portfolio, and your campaign can provide a valuable experience to display their skills. If you aren't that fortunate, consider hiring someone who can insure that the face of your campaign looks professional. If not possible, do your best to complete your own design using common computer software. You can even browse the internet for examples of other successful campaign logos so that you can develop a better understanding of what works. Remember, campaign materials will reflect your candidacy and if your materials look careless and unsystematic, voters may assume the same of you.

When developing your message for your campaign materials, keep in mind three principles: Quick, Informative, and Catchy. As discussed in the previous chapter, a candidate's message should be packaged so that readers can quickly relate to your message and remember it. Some campaign materials may offer the voter the opportunity to delve further into the message by providing details of your goals; however, most voters will not take the extra time to explore your agenda. For those who are curious and demand more precise explanations, they can flip through the available literature. The majority of campaign materials, however, should include the name of the candidate(s), with a quick message that conveys the campaign's core message.

When developing a core message, it is effective to develop a slogan that voters will remember. Your message should personify your strongest qualities while making a lasting impression on the voter. In the 1950's, President Eisenhower's campaign slogan was "I like Ike." This personified Eisenhower's trademark liability with a rhyming slogan that people could remember. Senator Barack Obama kept it very simple. In the 2008 presidential campaign, Obama's slogan was "Change." This was Obama's strength, since a majority of Americans felt America was on the wrong track. The political climate of your environment should dictate whether a candidate should take a light hearted or very direct approach.

Every campaign boils down to one question: Change versus more of the same. If you are challenging an incumbent or a member of the incumbent team, you should stress that the current team is not performing effectively in office and that there needs to be change. If you are the incumbent or part of the incumbent team holding the office you wish to acquire, it is beneficial to stress that the voters should allow you to stay the course. The old saying goes, "If it ain't broke, don't fix it."

Once you have constructed your core message and maybe even a campaign slogan, it is time to consider creating some campaign literature such as brochures, fliers, tri-folds, etc. The premise of literature is to provide your campaign's image and message to the voter on paper. Literature should be mass produced so that you can freely distribute it among the electorate. It is preferred to leave the design to someone trained in graphic design; however, this isn't always possible. There are a variety of free and cheap computer programs in which you can use to develop and print campaign literature. Printing can be expensive, and this is where a large portion of your budget should be directed. Consider your budgetary restraints when designing your material so that you can maximize your, often limited, budget.

Literature should be simple on its face and prominently display a candidate's name, as it would appear on the ballot. It should also display exactly what office the candidate is seeking, and a website to visit for more details. The only remaining item on the face of the literature or flier should be your slogan or packaged core message. All other details regarding your platform, your endorsement, or bios of your team should be kept off simple fliers and only included inside literature such as brochures or on your campaign website. Inundating your readers with too much information at first will overwhelm and distract them. If the reader likes what they see on the face of a brochure or a flier, they will likely seek out more information by opening the brochure or going to the website.

When developing your literature design, keep in mind that there are two extremes by which to measure. First there is the Wall Street Journal, which is very heavy on text, extremely drab, and contains little to no illustrations. The text is tightly packed onto the page in order to provide more information to the reader. The WSJ is confident that its average reader values the reporting and does not require flash. On the other side of the spectrum is the USA Today, which is full of vivid color, engaging photos, and info graphics throughout, which demand the reader's attention. While the Wall Street Journal has placed substance before style, the USA Today has made its living on putting style before substance. The winning combination likely falls closer to the USA Today, but that decision has to be made by you and your team depending on the audience you are trying to reach and the message you are attempting to deliver. It is up to you to strike the perfect balance between style and substance that will appeal to your particular electorate.

Campaign signs present your image to the mainstream electorate at your school. Since a large number of students will not fall into one of your target groups and will not have the opportunity to get to know you, the signs may be the only impression they have regarding your candidacy. And when they place their vote, those signs may be the only thing that comes to mind when they see your name. If your signs have created a positive image, your chances of winning that vote will increase dramatically.

Campaign signs are displays in which you will strategically place on campus so that students will see without exuding any effort whatsoever. These can be as small as yard signs that stick into the ground, to something as large as a billboard. Your election by-laws may have restrictions governing campaign signs, like how large they can be and where you can place them. The campaign manager or press secretary should internalize these rules and keep everyone abreast in order to avoid any unnecessary violations. Minor violations may seem inconsequential; yet if reported by the school newspaper, it could snowball into bad press. Always avoid controversy in an election. A small nugget of controversy can grow into a mountain of controversy on a slow news day, so avoid unnecessary risks by careful compliance with all election and school regulations.

At its best, campaign signs will positively brand your name, the office for which you are running, and possibly a brief message or slogan into the minds of voters. If, however, the signs are poorly designed and/or constructed, they could have an unfavorable effect. If a voter sees a sign which appears disorderly, substandard, or even incorrect; voters will carry this image with them into the polls and it is likely they will assume that this is exactly how you will perform if elected. This disaster can be avoided with careful planning and collective execution.

Paying for signs to be professionally produced could bring credibility; however, they can often be very expensive and consume the majority of your campaign budget. For students who have a limited budget, but do have some free time and a location to paint; homemade signs are more efficient. It gives the team a place to socialize and get to know one another while being productive. Buying plywood, paint, and brushes is more cost efficient than paying for signs to be professional made.

Here is a tip for making your own professional signs. Once you have completed the design for your sign by including your campaign insignia, the office for which you are running, and possibly your campaign slogan; upload the design on a laptop computer. Flip the design so that it is backward, using an option available on almost all software including Microsoft Word. Attach a projector to your computer and shine the image on the surface you are using for your sign. Adjust the distance and the focus until you have placed the image clearly and neatly onto the sign surface. Then use a construction pencil to trace the image onto the sign surface. It is helpful to paint the surface of the sign with the background color of your choice and let it dry before you begin your trace. Once the design is traced onto the surface, you can use small brushes to fill in the design.

There are advantages with professionally constructed signs. Time usually favors professional signs because you merely place the order and wait for them to be finished. During this time, you can be working on your long list of campaign tasks. Nonetheless, if the finished signs do not meet your liking, will you have time to have them remade? Also, unexpected things can happen which could back up production at the printing company, which could cause a costly delay to your campaign. At least with homemade signs, you are in full control of their production and can sleep well knowing it is in your hands.

Manufacturing campaign materials requires lots of time, hard work, and creativity. It also provides a wealth of experience to those pursuing a career in marketing, graphic art, business, advertising, or politics. Take advantage of those students who would benefit by inviting them to join your staff to produce presentable materials. Literature and slogans should be quick, informative, and catchy. Grabbing the voters' attention immediately is the key to campaign materials. Do not be afraid of a do-it-yourself method in order to meet your budget. It will allow you time to get to know your staff while using teamwork to be productive. Additionally, do not be afraid to create new and creative ways of distributing your message. Once your ammunition is ready, it is time to pound the pavement and win this election!

Chapter 12 — Message Delivery

Let's recap. You have made the tough decision to run for office, you have assessed your electorate, and you have assembled a staff. You have crafted a campaign timeline, raised the funds to finance your campaign, and determined the voting groups you will target. Additionally, you carefully crafted a platform, designed and constructed materials, and collected key endorsements. Each and every thing that you have done is preparation for the next few steps. It is time to make the pivot from preparation to execution.

In this chapter, you will learn how to use your skills to sell your campaign to the voters you previously targeted. You will reinforce your base while reaching out to swing voters by showing them that you are the best candidate for advancing their interests. You will brandish your endorsements to voters to illustrate to students that campus leaders trust and value your candidacy. Achieving all of this is impossible without implementing a carefully orchestrated plan. This chapter will guide you through drafting such a plan.

Campus elections will almost always regulate the time period in which candidates and their teams can actively campaign for office. This means that candidates are only permitted to campaign for a fixed period of time which begins when the election by-laws dictate. For instance, the University of Wisconsin — Milwaukee limits its SGA elections to seven days with no campaigning allowed on the two days of elections. The by-laws define campaigning as "any act that may directly or indirectly influence [students] to vote for a particular candidate or party." This is a typically broad regulation that prohibits all forms of campaigning until the election commissioner decides. Similarly, student candidates for campus-wide office at Metro State in Denver get six days to campaign for office until the elections.

Since campaigning is formally limited to a short amount of time, it is imperative to use that time effectively. Blitzkrieg is a German word meaning "lighting war" and is a phrase used to describe the German's style of war during WWII. Blitzkrieg was a devastating tactic based on speed and surprise. It was designed so that the enemy had no time or idea of how to create a defense, because they never knew when and where the next attack was coming. Blitzkrieg was performed in waves that would progressively soften the enemy over a short amount of time. Like the German Blitzkrieg of WWII, good campaigns work quickly, powerfully, and unpredictably to inform the electorate and overpower the opposing candidate. This chapter will demonstrate three phases of campaigning during the designated period in which you will work fast and efficiently to win the votes you need.

Phase One of delivering your message involves you and your team putting in place an infrastructure that lets students know that you are officially running for office. This is the official rollout of your entire campaign that should leave a positive impression on students, yet not overwhelm them. This will include erecting signs in high traffic areas so that students will see your name, what office you are seeking, and possibly a campaign slogan. It is important that this step begins at the very minute your election bylaws allow you to campaign, so that you do not miss getting the best locations for your signs on campus. By waiting, you give your opponents an unnecessary advantage. Speed is a key essential in Blitzkrieg, so a well-orchestrated plan of attack is essential. By breaking into teams, the canvassing can be done in a quick and efficient fashion. A strategic plan should be calculated well in advance and carefully communicated to the team before permission is given by the election commissioner to begin.

Example: At Atlantic State University (ASU), the official campaign period begins at the adjournment of the mandatory meeting held to certify each candidate for office at ASU. The candidate, Jarrod, attended the meeting and at the very moment of adjournment, sent a text message to Michelle, his sign coordinator. When Michelle received the message, she sent out a chain text to the three teams who were in position to canvass different sides of campus. The message also reached the web master who was waiting for the signal in order to go live with the campaign website. Within a half an hour of the meeting's adjournment, there were 15 large signs erected at each high traffic area, fliers posted on every bulletin board and entrances to academic buildings containing the campaign's website, and a website posted on the internet for the voter to access the issues. The next morning, students were greeted with professionally made campaign materials offering them an easy website address to access further information regarding their platform. By getting there first, Jarrod's team secured the best spots on campus for signs and fliers.

During Phase One, you will also begin meeting with your base organizations during their weekly meetings in order to reinforce support. These meetings should have been scheduled weeks in advance by your campaign manager, and the manager should brief you on any details about the meeting beforehand. When addressing these organizations, there may be a time limit given for which you should strictly adhere to. However, if there is not a limit, never take more than five to seven minutes, and always allow time for members to ask questions. The goal in these presentations is to be informative and appealing to the members. Use your elevator speech to present your platform, and prioritize the points according to the importance of the issues to the groups you are presenting. Always be respectful and thank the group for allowing you to take time out of their meeting.

Example: Jean is running for student council president. Her platform is three pronged to include: Improved Academics, Expanded Cafeteria, and Enhanced Security. On Monday, Jean is to meet with the Honors Society; and on Tuesday, with the Beta Beta Sorority located a few blocks from campus. The Honors Society is likely most interested in improving the school's academic opportunities, thus Jean should address this first and most often in order to appeal to this organization. Tuesday, however, Jean should begin her speech with the issue of security and her plan to add lighting and guards to monitor the areas around campus in order to make it safer for commuting students. Since Jean spoke with the leaders of each group earlier in the process, she knew these were areas each were concerned about.

The campaign's website and social pages should go live at the very minute the campaign officially begins. As stated previously, your signs and other material should include your campaign's internet address so that students can explore your campaign at their own discretion. Your staff and friends of the campaign can drastically improve your web presence in Phase One by doing a number of things including "liking" your Facebook page, "following" you on Twitter, posting links from your website and Facebook page on their Facebook page, and by Tweeting information about your campaign from their personal Twitter account. Social marketing has become the most effective way of marketing a campus campaign due to the use of computers and smart phones.

Phase Two should begin a few days into the official campaign period. This Phase increases the dosage of your message to the voters. More signs and fliers should be erected in high traffic areas, so that your name becomes increasingly familiar with voters without inundating them all at once. Students should start meeting you and your staff on campus, and voters should be given material which further explains the details of your platform.

By this point, you should be finishing up your organizational meetings with base organizations and making the pivot to focusing on swing groups. Although you are turning your attention to swing groups, it is imperative that you never do anything to risk losing any portion of your base vote. A good candidate will hold his base vote close even when reaching out to new groups. This is tricky balance that can trip up the best of candidates. As previously discussed, when you take drastic positions to appeal to your base voters, it may make it more difficult to appeal to swing voters. Never say or do anything that will risk your base; because without a foundation to stand on, you will surely fall.

Example: Tony is running for student body president at Lincoln College. Tony and his team have shored up the Campus Christian Club by making a campaign pledge to get funding for a new chapel on campus. During Phase Two, Tony decides to attend an annual Toga Party being held by the large fraternity Kappa Pi, who is also one of Tony's identified swing groups. In an effort to appeal to the Kappa's, Tony leads them in a traditional fraternity chant. The chant is offensive and contains several curse words and even uses God's name in vein. When it gets back to the Campus Christian Club, they hold a vote and denounce their support of Tony.

Increased personal interaction with voters is a cornerstone of Phase Two. The candidate and other team members will be spending time each day in high traffic areas interacting with voters. This interaction will include asking students for their vote. If your campaign personally asks for a student's vote and the opposition does not, there is a good chance that that student will place a vote with you. The most impactful ask comes from the actual candidate, who should be in the busiest area of campus to reach the most voters. If there is a vice-presidential candidate, this candidate should also be pounding the pavement meeting voters in high traffic areas. Additionally, team members should be handing out campaign literature such as brochures. Lastly, it is important that team members remember to tell supportive students when, where, and how to vote. It is useless to win someone's support if they are not educated on how to place their vote. In the next chapter, we will discuss how to Get Out the Vote on the days of the election; yet it is important to inform voters as early and often as possible.

In addition to informing general voters on when, where, and how to vote; it is a good idea to designate someone to educate your base organizations on voting. This designee should hold a meeting with representatives from each base organization to review their plan for voting, and create one if they do not. Perhaps a plan could be made for everyone to mobilize to the polls together. Your campaign team should provide a one-pager with instructions on how to vote, including what will be needed at the polls and exactly when and where to go.

Phase Two also includes ramping up your online presence. Your website visits should be increasing exponentially with voters visiting to find out more about your campaign. If visits are not increasing, this must be addressed. The amount of Facebook "Likes" should also be increasing drastically. You should be sending out status updates two to three times daily to keep supporters informed on your campaign and instructions on how to vote. Lastly, your list

of followers on Twitter should be increasing dramatically and your staff and supporters should be "Tweeting" about your campaign even more than in Phase One. Remember to use uniform hash tags when tweeting for the campaign.

Phase Three is the final and most fully involved stage of your campaign, which will extend to election day(s). At this stage, your campaign should be hitting on all cylinders. The candidate and team members should be spending long hours each day on campus handing out marketing materials, asking for votes, and educating supporters on how to vote. Your focus should be reaching deep into the swing vote, while staying true to your base supporters.

Some school election bylaws, such as University of Wisconsin — Milwaukee prohibit campaigning on the days of the election. If your school has the same prohibition, Phase Three is your last chance to talk to voters, and you should distribute all marketing materials in this phase. Regardless, this stage of the campaign focuses on ensuring that your base voters mobilize to the polls, while you continue to appeal to swing voters. Ideally, your Letters to the Editor will published during this period in order to have the most impact on undecided voters.

In Phase Three, the campaign manager should be rushing to find events for the candidate to attend, to appeal to swing voters when the candidate is not on campus talking to voters. This period is a sprint nearing the end of a marathon, and the candidate and campaign manager will likely get little rest. A candidate's schedule should be dictated by the campaign manager, and stuffed full from morning to night during Phase Three.

On the internet front, numbers should be continuing to increase. The entire team will be constantly directing students to the website and the social networking sites. The sites should focus on voter education during this phase. The front page of the website should include simple instructions on when, where, and how to vote. If your campus offers online voting, the campaign webpage should offer a link to the school's voting page, if permitted. Your Facebook page should include status updates that include instructions on when, where, and how to vote. You should be tweeting about voting instructions, and these should be re-tweeted by team members and close supporters.

Delivering your message is the key to winning; nevertheless, keep in mind that this book does not intend to tell you exactly what to do, but merely illustrates a structure in which you may follow. Each candidate should have their own creative ideas to implement, and it is encouraged to incorporate your ideas within each phase of the Blitzkrieg. The marketing tactics included in the phases presented are merely suggestions in which you may add and subtract, depending on your preference. Use this book sparingly and design a strategy that best works for you. Winning will require you to be efficient with often limited and precious time.

Chapter 13 — Get Out the Vote (GOTV)

A candidate can decide to run, assemble an all-star staff, construct the perfect message, clearly deliver that message to each and every voter, but still lose unless voters get to the polls and actually vote. Convincing the voters that you are the best candidate is only half the battle; the other half is mobilizing them to the polls to cast that winning vote. Everything you have done before now is simply preparing you for this stage. This is your one chance to get it right, and this chapter shows you how to close the deal.

In today's fast pace times, voters stay extremely busy and must prioritize their daily tasks. College students are especially busy juggling their classes, studies, and work. It is also a priority to most college students to maintain a social life which is essential to the college culture. When prioritizing tasks, students usually place academics and socializing ahead of voting in school elections. As important as you may view your own campaign, it is not likely high on the to-do list of your fellow students. Without some convincing, students are not likely to believe that any elected student official is going to improve or even affect their daily lives. With a well-orchestrated plan that takes these factors into consideration and works to convince students that voting for you is quick, easy, and fun; you can defeat apathy and win.

The procedures to vote are different at every school, and

it is very important to know these procedures early and educate your entire team on them. While some schools work to make it easier for students to vote by providing amenities such as online voting, multiple voting days, and even multiple voting locations; others take a more conservative approach. Single day voting at one single location is still common among American schools. Your school's voting arrangements will dictate the kind of GOTV plan to which you will implement.

When crafting a GOTV strategy, remember that it is not helpful to inundate voters with too many voting instructions all at once. Alternatively, gradually increase the amount of voting instructions as you get closer to the election. From the earliest stage, campaign materials should prominently display what day the election is taking place, so that students will be told early and often when to vote. As the election nears, students will be ready for more information, such as where they need to go to vote and what hours the polls will be open. This can be distributed in a number of ways including (but not limited to) leaflets, campus signs or fliers, door knocks at dormitories, emails, or other social networking sites. You should even consider countdown clocks, since voters will often develop a sense of urgency if they are reminded that time is running out on them. This can be done on signs, websites, on social networking sites, or with sidewalk chalk on campus. Be creative and resourceful.

Another tactic of early GOTV is making voting plans with key constituency groups. It is never a good idea to assume anything, so assuming that a valued base group will vote can lead to disappointment. Remember, students are busy and easily distracted. Consider assigning a team member to each of these voting groups to ensure that they have a plan, educate the members on that plan, and execute the plan on election day(s). This will usually require contacting the leadership of the group, at least a few weeks before the election to ensure that the election is on their organization calendars, and that there is not a conflicting obligation that will keep them from voting. If the group does not have a voting plan, recommend one that will not inconvenience the group. On election day, it is this designee's responsibility to make sure their respective groups get to the polls and place their vote for you. Unfortunately, some voting groups have no natural organization. This requires your team to be creative and resourceful in mobilizing these students to the polls.

Example: Mitch is a candidate, and is running to be the student representative on the school's Board of Trustees at his college. One of Mitch's base organizations is the Performing Arts Club (PAC), due to Mitch's participation in the group as an underclassman. Because Mitch depends on the support of the PAC to win the election, he appointed Amanda as the person accountable for getting PAC to the polls. Although Amanda served as the graphic designer for the campaign, her duties as graphic designer were complete, and she was available to help in the GOTV efforts. Three weeks before the election, Amanda contacted the PAC president and asked if PAC would include the election on its events calendar, and if the president would remind PAC members to vote for Mitch. Additionally, Amanda worked with the president to make voting plans in which groups would leave from the Theater Department every hour to walk to the Student Union to vote. On the day of the election, Amanda and the PAC president stayed at the Theater Department and organized group walks to the Student Union. After each student voted, they were given a sticker to wear indicating that they had voted. Those in the Theater Department without voting stickers were approached by the PAC president and Amanda for some encouragement to vote.

When there is a lack of organization within a group of voters, or you are having trouble enticing voting groups to commit to voting, consider creating your own events to attract students to the polls. Students can be motivated by different things, such as free food, sporting events, or purely social outings. Three things to remember if you plan an event to attract your supporters to the polls: 1) It is not wise to spend large sums of campaign funds on these events, because these funds are better used on materials to win the support of voters. 2) If you plan to offer some kind of free item or service to students for coming out to vote, be sure to award them after they actually vote. If you do not, you run the risk of giving away things to students without the verification that they have or will go the polls. Poll workers will often distribute a sticker to those who have voted. If not, your volunteers can distribute stickers or give voters tickets as they leave the polling location. Be careful not to be too exclusive here. Since you do not know who voted for you and who did not, err on the side of caution by including everyone. 3) Do not use this event as a way of attracting new supporters, but rather to mobilize those who are already supporters. Students who think you are buying their vote, with a mere freebie, will likely question your integrity.

Example: It is election day at George Marshall College, and students have two choices for student body president: Dixon and Jasper. While Jasper used his $500 budget to make campaign signs and literature to reach out to his targeted voters, Dixon saved his entire budget to hold a huge barbeque on election day. The barbeque was held on the quad near the polling center, and was open to any student who wanted to come and have a meal paid for by the Dixon Campaign. While Jasper was trying to find ways to mobilize his base groups to the polls, he realized that his opponent's barbeque was a perfect attraction. Jasper encouraged all of his base groups to go the Dixon barbeque and enjoy a free meal before going to place a vote for him.

Jasper's supporters were the first students at the event. They all enjoyed a delicious meal from Dixon and then made their way to the polls. On their way to the poll, they were greeted by Jasper who had a sign that said, "Wash down you BBQ with a refreshing glass of VOTE FOR JASPER." His supporters thanked him for the notification of the barbeque and quickly went to place a vote for Jasper.

Another way to organize and mobilize groups who have trouble organizing internally is to simply go to them to educate and encourage them to vote. This could be done by email, social networking, phone calls, or just simple door knocks with fliers. If these groups assemble, find out where and when so that you can address them together. These efforts must always be calculated so that you avoid mobilizing your opponent's voters. Remember, GOTV is about mobilizing your identified supporters, not winning the support of new voters. By simply blanketing students this close to the election, you run the risk of guiding your opponent's voters to the polls to place a vote against you.

Example: On the night before the big election at Faber College, Sandy sent out her two most outgoing volunteers, Jerome and Eric, to blanket the east side of campus. Sandy was the campaign manager and she decided that the higher the turnout, the better her candidate's chances were. Jerome and Eric took to the dorms, where they came upon the school's hockey team returning from practice. Eric explained to the team that the following day was election day, and he gave them all of the relevant details. After that, Jerome began randomly handing out fliers to students as they walked in the dorms, reminding them of how, when, and where to vote. What Sandy did not realize was that her opponent, Aaron, used to live in that dorm and had won the support of the hockey team and most of the residents. Thus, it is likely that Jerome and Eric had just mobilized their competitor's voters to the polls.

This kind of damage is easily avoidable if you and your team are aware that GOTV is about mobilizing supporters, not winning new support. Your team must be cognizant of what voting groups you are aiming to mobilize to the polls. While you should never discourage anyone from voting, it is not your responsibility to educate your opponent's supporters, but it is essential to your success that you mobilize your own. Only the candidate should be vying for additional supporters once the election time has come. The rest of the team should be ensuring that the base and swing voters are taking the time to vote. Without a good showing from your base at the polls, your chances of winning decrease drastically.

Although emails and social networking are effective in spreading the message of your campaign and disseminating important voting instructions when you simply cannot reach these voters in person; personal interaction is always preferred. When someone hands you something and delivers a personal message, the message is more lasting than that of an electronic message or a sign. If done correctly, personal interaction can be intimate and make a lasting impression on a voter. Not only can it educate them on how to vote, it can win or reinforce their support of you or your candidate. Additionally, avoid passing out literature close to a trash can. Although it is expected that voters will throw your literature away, the hope is that they will keep it long enough to read it.

Social media is a terrific tool for mobilizing voters because it allows you to reach the masses with minimal effort. Facebook and Twitter messages spread like a virus if executed correctly. By now, your campaign should have a large number of Facebook "likes" and Twitter "followers." By disseminating voting information in the form of Facebook posts and tweets, campaigns can educate their base groups about when, where, and how to vote for their candidate. And since many organizations have their own Facebook page, your campaign's Facebook administrator can post directly on the page. This means all members of this base organization will get a notification to your post; most likely directly to their smart phones!

When election time has arrived, your campaign should go into "All hands on deck" mode. The entire team should be active and dedicated exclusively to GOTV. Ideally, every campaign will have a GOTV director to craft your team's plan early in the campaign. If your campaign is short on volunteers, consider delegating this responsibility out to one of your more trusted workers. The campaign manager, GOTV director, and the candidate should settle on an election day(s) plan at least a week before the polls open.

On election day(s), the GOTV director should be in a "War Room." This means a quiet room where the GOTV director can operate without any distractions. The director should have two phones, in case one fails. She/he should have a laptop computer with two chargers. It is also helpful, but not required, to have dry erase boards in order to make necessary notes throughout the day. Preferably, the room would be located in the heart of campus, so that the GOTV director can be deployed into action in emergency situations. Unless an emergency occurs, the GOTV director should be in the War Room directing traffic over the phone in accordance to a plan previously agreed to by the candidate and the campaign manager. This plan should include periodic reports that should be completed and given to the GOTV director throughout election day(s).

While the director is in the War Room, the others should be delegated into groups in which they will be accountable for mobilizing to the polls. The delegates are the ones who will be reporting directly to the GOTV director while the polls remain open. Since these roles can be time consuming, it is important that the GOTV director has all shifts covered with written commitments from volunteers. Missing shifts could cost the campaign countless votes, so it is important to get these filled early and even have reserve volunteers scheduled to deploy if needed. Remember to delegate your most trusted team members to your most valued base and swing groups. Delegates should have some form of reporting to the GOTV director so that progress can be assessed. If resources need to be shifted, this is the only way the GOTV director will know to take action. When possible, delegates should have checklists of the names of members of particular voting groups so that they can simply check them off throughout the day(s).

Students who are not delegates assigned to mobilizing valued voting groups, should be working the lines. Voting lines are often long, and can be unattractive to busy and easily distracted students. It is the job of the line workers to ensure that your supporters stay in line and do not leave. When you have won the support of a voter and successfully mobilized that voter to the polls, it is senseless and costly to lose them because of the wait time. Line workers do whatever is necessary, within the rules, to keep these supporters in the voting line. This may require giving them water if it is hot, hot chocolate if it is cold, or even entertainment if they are bored. Line workers are creative, candid, and do whatever it takes to close the deal on votes.

While the GOTV director is directing people behind the scenes, the campaign manager is managing people on the ground, the delegates are mobilizing valued groups, and the line workers are at the polls working the lines; the candidate(s) should be in a high traffic area asking for votes. This is the campaigns last chance to win over any undecided voters. And while the majority of the team should be mobilizing supporters, the candidate(s) should be pounding the pavement for every last vote. Though exhausting, the candidate must continue to ask for each and every vote, while being prepared to answer tough questions from potential voters. The candidate should also prominently display his or her name near where he/she is standing throughout the day, so that voters clearly know who you are. This can be done by standing near a large sign or by wearing a campaign t-shirt. Do not rely on the fliers being distributed because there will be many who walk by without receiving any material, but may see your prominent sign and/or shirt.

When all duties have been assigned, it is possible that you will have additional volunteers who need assignments. These volunteers should be given one of two assignments: Sign waver or blind door knocker. A sign waver will deploy to an area that contains a high number of your base supporters, and that is preferably a high traffic location. Sign wavers will hold signs with your campaign logo and some information about how to vote. Blind door knockers will canvass areas where your base voters live. They will knock on doors and inform students on how, when, and where to go vote for your candidate. These practices run the risk of mobilizing your opponent's voters, so be diligent in assigning locations. These assignments should only be delegated if you have a surplus of volunteers.

Be careful, some schools do prohibit campaigning of any sort on the days the polls are open. If this is the case, do not ask for votes. Furthermore, find out early if you are able to work to mobilize voters and whether or not it is considered campaigning if you are working in a non-partisan way to get voters to the polls. Do not rely on your own interpretation, because you could be risking the hard work of everyone on your team.

Your campaign may attract volunteers who are aspiring lawyers, pre-laws students, and even law students. These future jurists will enjoy contributing by lending their legal skills to your campaign. Inasmuch, voter protection is an important part of campaigns because it oversees and secures students' ability to place a vote for the candidate of their choice. On election day, the voter protection volunteer(s) will be present at the polls to ensure that the proper procedures are followed by poll workers. The campaign manager should arrange a meeting with the supervisor of elections or election commissioner in order to approve this practice. Prior to election day, the voter protection volunteer will be working to fully understand voting procedures and to educate students on exactly what they will need to know to vote on election day. This importance of a voter protection presence is escalated if your campus practices electronic or online voting.

Online elections have become more prevalent, especially on college campuses. Regardless of the method of placing votes, the principles and strategies will remain the same. Your tactics may change, yet you are still striving to reach the same goal. Online voting is relatively new and will require you and your team to use creative tactics which work within the rules put forth by your school.

Election day is chaotic and unpredictable. Although you have a solid game plan that each of your volunteers can fully understand; things could change at the drop of a hat.If your plan is not working and deviation is required, the campaign manager must be ready to make that call. Additionally, volunteers must be trained to understand this dynamic. It is imperative that volunteers be flexible and ready to change roles upon command in order to do what is needed to win. Although quick and unplanned change is frustrating and chaotic, it is a part of campaigning and should be accepted if not welcomed by the entire campaign staff.

Example: The campaign to elect Amir as President of the Student Bar at Coastal Law School has gone as smoothly as anyone could have predicted. He won the coveted endorsements of the school's Moot Court Team and the Federalists Law Students. These groups traditionally make up 60% of the vote. One hour into election day, the campaign manager gets word that a Supreme Court Justice has made a surprise visit to the neighboring town, and has scheduled to meet with the Coastal Moot Court Team. This meant that the entire Moot Court Team was being bused seventy miles away and would not return until after the polls have closed. An hour later, the campaign manager is informed that the Federalists have announced that they are pulling their support for Amir after becoming aware that Amir is personally involved with a political group which advocates for strict new gun laws. Two hours into the election and Amir's campaign plan of mobilizing these two groups has become irrelevant. Furthermore, the one polling location on campus has been moved to a different building!

The campaign manager and Amir know that they must change directions and do it quickly. The volunteers who were given the task of mobilizing the Federalists were called and reassigned to working to mobilize the Moot Court Team to the polls before their bus left to see the Supreme Court Justice. The campaign manager even persuades the Moot Court coach to direct the bus to pick up the team at the polling location, which gave the members more time to vote before leaving town. Furthermore, Amir makes a phone call to Law Students for Gun Sensibility and tells them what happened with the Federalists and asks for their full support. When they agree to support Amir, the campaign manager assigns volunteers to begin making calls, emails, and social networking posts to members of the gun group to mobilize them to the polls. Meanwhile, other volunteers are tweeting supporters about the new voting location. Other volunteers were brought onto the campus to pass out hundreds of fliers indicating the new voting location and asking for a vote for Amir.

Amir's campaign had every reason to be complacent and enjoy the smooth ride of election day. The heavy lifting had been done, and sufficient support had been given to Amir. Campaigns, however, are fickle and anything can happen. Amir and his staff were trained to be flexible and never complacent and comfortable. They were ready when the plan changed and because of it, they were able to craft and execute a new plan on the fly.

When the clock expires on election day(s), your work is temporarily done. Weeks or even months of hard work have ended and as odd as it seems, it is finally time to relax. Take this time to bring your staff together and thank them. Win or lose, they had the confidence in you to donate their blood, sweat, and tears for weeks or even months. Speak to them from the heart and try to calm them before the results are announced. Waiting for results is very intense and stressful, so it is very important to do something to keep your mind occupied while you wait.

When receiving the results, it is advantageous to appear calm and collected although you may be very nervous and unsure. Your supporters will adopt the same demeanor in which you display; so if you are calm and confident, they will be calm and confident. Be thankful to everyone involved and express that you appreciate being able to be involved in such an educational and diplomatic process. When the results are released, be patient and polite, and be respectful to your opponent, even in defeat. This means you should reserve your reactions, whether celebratory or disappointment, until you have left the presence of your opponent, the press, and constituents, and have reconvened with your team. For Sample Election Day Plan, *see Appendix G.*

Sample Election Day Plan

48 Hour Plan for Student Body Presidential Campaign at Fake College

(a) GOTV (Day 1)

(i) Candidate

1. 8-10 a.m. — Sign waving Greek Row
2. 10-12 p.m. — Door canvassing at Greek Row
3. 12-1 p.m. — Dorm Cafeteria A
4. 2-4 p.m. Blind Canvassing University Apts.
5. 4-6 — Dorm Cafeteria B
6. 7-9 — Basketball game Gate A/B

(ii) Management

1. Campaign manager at headquarters managing candidate/workers

(iii) Door Canvassers

— two rounds 10 a.m. & 12 p.m. (Targeted)

1. Alex — Fraternity Row
2. Betty — Sorority Houses
3. Ellen — Sorority Houses
4. Frank — University Apts.

(iv) Phone Canvassers

— 10-4 p.m. (Targeted)

1. Andy 10-1 a.m. at HQ
2. Brenda 1-4 p.m. at HQ

(v) Flier passers

1. Anthony—8-10 a.m. & 11-1 p.m. in Cafeteria of Dorm A
2. Beth—8-12 p.m. in College of Business atrium
3. Carl—12-4 p.m. in College of Business atrium
4. Denise—6-9 p.m. at Basketball game Gate A
5. Ed—6-9 p.m. at Basketball game Gate B

(vi) E-mailers

1. Art—8 a.m. & 12 p.m.

(vii) Sign Wavers

1. Ann—8-11 a.m. university entrance
2. Ben—12-4 p.m. university entrance
3. Clark—8-11 a.m. Greek row
4. Dana—12-4 p.m. Greek row

(b) GOTV (Day 2)

(i) Candidate

1. 7-9 a.m.—Sign waving at university entrance
2. 9-10 a.m.—Sign waving at Greek Row
3. 10-11:30 a.m.—Door Canvass at Greek Row
4. 11:30-12 p.m.—Lunch and meet/greet at Dorm Cafeteria A
5. 12-2 p.m.—Pass out fliers on campus (near polling booth A)
6. 2-5 p.m.—Pass out fliers on campus (near polling booth B)
7. 5-7 p.m.—Dinner meet/greet at Cafeteria B

(ii) Management

1. At headquarters managing

(iii) Voter Protection

1. April — 8 a.m. — 5 p.m. at Polling Booth A
2. Baxter — 8 a.m. — 5 p.m. at Polling Booth B

(iv) Door Canvassers,

three rounds 10 a.m., 12 p.m., 2 p.m. (Targeted)

1. Alex — Fraternity Row
2. Betty — Sorority Houses
3. Ellen — Sorority Houses
4. Frank — University Apts.

(v) Phone Canvassers

— 10-4 p.m. (Targeted)

1. Andy 10-1 a.m. at HQ
2. Brenda 1-4 p.m. at HQ
3. Anthony — 8-10 a.m. & 11-1 p.m. in Cafeteria of Dorm A
4. Beth — 8-12 p.m. in College of Business atrium
5. Carl — 12-4 p.m. in College of Business atrium
6. Denise — 6-9 p.m. at Basketball game Gate A
7. Ed — 6-9 p.m. at Basketball game Gate B

(vi) E-mailers

1. Art — 8 a.m. & 12 p.m.

(vii) Sign Wavers

1. Ann — 8-11 a.m. university entrance
2. Ben — 12-4 p.m. university entrance
3. Clark — 8-11 a.m. Greek row
4. Dana — 12-4 p.m. Greek row

(viii) 5pm Polls close

1. Everyone report to HQ

Conclusion

This book is a useful resource and provides you with the guidance you need to run a competent and competitive campaign at your school. Each chapter addresses an important aspect of a school campaign, and when applicable, each phase should be properly considered. Use the examples and illustrations provided to internalize the concepts, tactics, and strategies presented in this book. When you are able to grasp these concepts and properly execute them, you will run an effective school campaign.

Your decision to run for student office should be carefully examined so that you are using your time, effort, and money efficiently. There are several factors to consider when making this decision, and each one should be examined independently. Review these factors with close friends or family so that you can get an alternate perspective on each area listed. After careful analysis of the factors, you should be able to make an educated decision on whether or not to become a candidate.

Once you have made the decision to throw your hat in the ring, it is important to begin understanding your electorate. By understanding your electorate's demographics, you will be in a better position to move forward in assembling a staff and designing a platform. Without a careful analysis of the electorate, you rely on assumptions and run the risk of an aimless campaign. To avoid this, keep your finger on the pulse of those who will be voting in your election.

Campaigns are made up of a series of time-sensitive tasks and deadlines. In order to manage them, it is advantageous to craft a campaign timeline which compartmentalizes the time you have before the election. Work backwards and enter all of your known deadlines on a calendar so that your campaign can keep an eye on deadlines in order to maintain focus on the appropriate areas. The core staff of a campaign should have easy access to a campaign calendar, and receive sufficient reminders of upcoming deadlines from the campaign manager.

Once the essential preliminary work has been addressed, it is time to assemble a core campaign staff. These core members consist of a campaign manager, a vice-presidential candidate (when applicable), and a finance director or treasurer. Choosing someone for each of these core positions will require specific considerations for the candidate. If a trusted campaign manager is chosen first, that manager can help you with the selection of other core team members. Consider the totality of the factors listed in Chapter 4 when making a knowledgeable selection.

The truth of politics is that effective campaigns cost money. In order to get your message dispersed to voters, money must be spent on those delivery methods. No matter how resourceful and frugal you may be, capital must be raised. Schools usually cap the amount of money a candidate can spend on a campaign, so it is imperative to know what your school's election by-laws require. If the candidate and core members are unable to fund the campaign internally, your campaign should reach out to relatives and friends for donations. Use other creative methods if necessary, but remember to be cautious and aware of the campaign finance rules at your school.

In Chapter 2, you built a basic understanding of your school's diverse demographics. At this point, the core members will work together to identify base, swing, and waste voters. Your base voters will make up your foundation voters, who will vote and support your candidacy. Swing voters are undecided and up for the taking, while waste voters will not vote for you. Waste voters may be supporters of your competitor, or possibly just possess values that conflict with those of your campaign. Regardless, your campaign should not spend resources reaching out to waste voters, but just those groups identified as base and swing voters. Ample time should be spent analyzing each identified voting group, and giving them a score so that the campaign can use its limited resources efficiently.

Although core team members will do the majority of the heavy lifting of the campaign, there will likely be others who want to volunteer to help you. Since there is plenty of work to be done, it is wise to bring in additional members and give them official campaign titles. There are several positions that are essential to larger campaigns; such as a press secretary, graphics coordinator, and a digital director. Instead of limiting your hires to those close to you, spend time to find qualified students who are willing to gain experience and can hit the ground running.

The candidate and those on the campaign team must always maintain a positive image in order to meet the high standard that voters have for elected officials. It should be understood that the candidate will be under the spotlight at all times during the campaign and the campaign manager must keep a close eye on what the candidate is doing so that he/she can make any corrective action when needed. Other members, although not as scrutinized, should be addressed and monitored so that they do not embarrass the campaign. The general rule should be: Do not do anything you would not want published on the front page of the school paper.

In order to reach out to your base and swing voters with the team you have assembled, you will design a platform and strategic plan of attack. This plan is the blueprint of your campaign. It is what will be used to electrify your base voters, and at the same time attract swing voters to your side. A platform should be simple so that students can quickly understand your core principles and basic plan with little effort. Address issues that are proven to be important to the voting groups you have targeted to win.

Many undecided voters trust the judgment of someone who has previously earned their confidence. If your candidacy is endorsed by influential people and the endorsement is prominently and timely displayed, it can help solidify your base while possibly attracting swing votes to your campaign. Your campaign should work to identify those people who are influential within your targeted groups and make the hard ask for their support. Once support is secured, a list of endorsements should be displayed in a clear manner on campaign materials.

The image of your campaign should be reflected in all of your campaign materials and internet presence. This could include anything from signs and fliers to websites and social media pages. For many voters, these outlets will be how they judge your candidacy and how you will perform as their representative. Efficient and succinct campaign materials and web presence will project that you and your team are also efficient and succinct. Whether you make your own campaign materials and websites or you pay to have them made, it is essential to plan ahead so that your materials are ready to be distributed and presented as soon as your school allows you to do so.

Once you have been given the green light, you and your team will execute delivering your message to the electorate. A solid plan is one that does not inundate students immediately, but one that builds gradually so that students are fed small bites of information progressively. Inundation will overwhelm voters, but a gradual flow of information about your campaign will create curiosity and leave voters wanting more. Your plan will work to secure your base votes while reaching out to your swing voters with an attractive campaign message, through various campaign methods.

The development of an effective message, and flawless execution of the delivery, mean nothing unless your constituents physically place a vote for you. By assuming a supporter will place a vote, you put your entire campaign at risk. Your campaign should have a GOTV plan that targets base supporters and swing voters to ensure that they mobilize to the polls on the day(s) of the election. This effort requires everyone on your campaign team to fulfill an important role. It is your job to ensure that each team member is well-versed on their role, and that they have everything needed to be successful.

Campaigns are complex and require countless hours of planning and labor. If you follow the steps provided in this book, you will not be overwhelmed; and you can, at the very least, be competitive in your campaign for student political office.